# Cambridge Elements ☰

Elements in Austrian Economics
edited by
Peter Boettke
*George Mason University*

# THE POLITICAL ECONOMY OF TERRORISM, COUNTERTERRORISM, AND THE WAR ON TERROR

Anne R. Bradley
*The Fund for American Studies*

Christopher J. Coyne
*George Mason University*

Abigail R. Hall
*University of Tampa*

CAMBRIDGE
UNIVERSITY PRESS

Shaftesbury Road, Cambridge CB2 8EA, United Kingdom

One Liberty Plaza, 20th Floor, New York, NY 10006, USA

477 Williamstown Road, Port Melbourne, VIC 3207, Australia

314–321, 3rd Floor, Plot 3, Splendor Forum, Jasola District Centre,
New Delhi – 110025, India

103 Penang Road, #05–06/07, Visioncrest Commercial, Singapore 238467

Cambridge University Press is part of Cambridge University Press & Assessment,
a department of the University of Cambridge.

We share the University's mission to contribute to society through the pursuit of
education, learning and research at the highest international levels of excellence.

www.cambridge.org
Information on this title: www.cambridge.org/9781108724081
DOI: 10.1017/9781108682534

First published 2023

*A catalogue record for this publication is available from the British Library.*

ISBN 978-1-108-72408-1 Paperback
ISSN 2399-651X (online)
ISSN 2514-3867 (print)

# The Political Economy of Terrorism, Counterterrorism, and the War on Terror

Elements in Austrian Economics

DOI: 10.1017/9781108682534
First published online: August 2023

Anne R. Bradley
*The Fund for American Studies*

Christopher J. Coyne
*George Mason University*

Abigail R. Hall
*University of Tampa*

**Author for correspondence:** Christopher J. Coyne, ccoyne3@gmu.edu

**Abstract:** This Element explores the topics of terrorism, counterterrorism, and the US government's war on terror following the September 11, 2001 terror attacks. It draws on insights from Austrian and public choice economics. First, it discusses the foundations of the economics of terrorism, emphasizing that the behaviors of terrorists and counterterrorists are purposeful and goal-oriented. It then considers the economics of counterterrorism policies and the importance of institutional change for reducing demand for terrorism. Next, it focuses on three dilemmas facing liberal societies in relation to counterterrorism efforts. The Element then provides an assessment of the US government's war on terror. It discusses the origins of the war, whether it can be judged a success or a failure, and some of the main effects both abroad and within the United States. The Element concludes by putting forward several areas for future research.

**Keywords:** counterterrorism, democracy, economics, terrorism, September 11, war on terror, liberalism, institutions, public choice

ISBNs: 9781108724081 (PB), 9781108682534 (OC)
ISSNs: 2399-651X (online), 2514-3867 (print)

# Contents

# 1 Introduction

Terrorism – use of unlawful violence to impart fear – is as old as history itself (Laqueur, 1987; Law, 2015, 2016; Chaliand and Blin, 2016). "Modern" terrorism finds its roots in the wake of the French Revolution and the Jacobins – the most influential and extreme political group of the period. With Maximilien Robespierre as the main public figure, they instituted what is now known as the "Reign of Terror," a period marked by extreme violence and the persistent threat thereof. "[While] fixated on eliminating as many people as possible who could challenge the new revolutionary order," writes Randall Law (2020: 87, emphasis added), "Robespierre and his colleagues understood they could not kill them all. Hence, this *policy of terror was intended to destroy those enemies who fell into the government's clutches and intimidate the rest,* even if they had not yet committed an overt act of counter-revolution." Writing elsewhere about the Reign of Terror, Law (2009: 62–63) states: "[W]e could say that the Terror was perversely educational since a primary goal was to shape the mind and behavior of the populace. This was the advent of modern terrorism, if not in form, then in function."

Though the world has experienced terrorism for ages, the seemingly unending, intensive focus on the topic is more contemporary. The attacks on the World Trade Center and the Pentagon on September 11, 2001, and the ensuing twenty-year "War on Terror," have prompted policymakers, scholars, and the general public to think about terrorism as never before. Since 9/11, thousands of articles in economics, sociology, psychology, military studies, and other disciplines explore issues related to the topic. Even a cursory search reveals the absolute explosion of research on the subject. Between 2018 and 2021 alone, at least 9,700 academic articles on the topic were published. If we look over the same period, more than 21.2 million popular press articles discuss terrorism.[1] This does not include the myriad television and news broadcasts, podcasts, and other media dedicated to the topic. For those alive in the period after 9/11, terrorism – and the policies intended to thwart it – is everywhere. From added security at movie theaters, sports arenas, and the airport, to increasingly alarmist television news broadcasts and speeches, press conferences, and debates by elected officials, discussions of terrorism, the impacts of terrorist activities, and the war against it are now an ever-present feature of daily life for many around the world. Whether we are traveling, banking, or just watching television, the war on terror permeates everyday life (see Coyne and Hall, 2021).

---

[1] Review of articles on Google Scholar related to "terrorism" narrowed by date.

Within economics, research on terrorism falls into two main categories.[2] One of these strands of literature engages with the study of terrorism from a *microeconomic* perspective, analyzing the choices faced by individual actors (see, for example, Pape, 2003). The second strand of literature takes a *macroeconomic* approach to exploring terrorism, examining how aggregate factors such as high unemployment and low economic growth correspond to outcomes related to terrorism (see, for example, Shughart, 2011).

Within the microeconomic vein, several themes and important insights emerge. Despite popular narratives that those engaged in terrorist activity are prone to mental illness, scholars agree that mental illness does not properly define terrorist behavior (Caplan, 2006; Shughart, 2011; Capellan, 2015). Similarly, despite frequent discussions of a "common" terrorist profile, research has not found any systematic way to describe terrorist actors – including both terrorism more broadly and suicide terrorism more specifically (see Pape, 2003 and Bhui, James, and Wessely, 2016).

Although the theory is not without dispute (Abrahms, 2008), rational choice economists within the microeconomic literature provide important evidence that terrorists operate as *rational actors* (Kydd and Walter, 2006). That is, terrorist actors undertake terrorism activities to obtain some end – an ideological or a political goal (Crenshaw, 1981; Enders and Sandler, 2000; Berman, 2003; Pape, 2003; Wintrobe, 2006; Hoffman and McCormick, 2004; Sandler and Enders, 2004; Anderton and Carter, 2005; Berman and Laitin, 2005; Caplan, 2006; Iannaccone, 2006; Shughart, 2006, 2011; Sprinzak, 2009; Sandler, 2015), financial reward, elevated status, or greater access to social services or education that is otherwise inaccessible (Zakaria, 2003). Like other actors facing scarcity, terrorists respond to their given environments, weigh the perceived costs and benefits when considering terrorist activity, and select action plans from their given choice set (Berman and Laitin, 2005; Caplan, 2006; Abrahms, 2008). Considering the relative costs associated with terrorist activities, terrorist perpetrators decide not only whether or not to participate but also their degree of involvement. While avoiding active participation may lessen the physical costs of a failed attack, it also weakens the individual's claim to first pick of the bounty in the event of success (Shughart, 2011).

While certain factors may alter terrorists' cost–benefit calculations, efforts to define macro-level, universal economic determinants of terrorism – such as poverty, demographics, and so on – have largely failed when controlling for institutional and political factors (Krieger and Meierrieks, 2011). While failed

---

[2] For literature reviews of the scholarship on the economics of terrorism and counterterrorism, see Bueno de Mesquita (2008), Schneider, Brück, and Meierrieks (2014), and Gaibulloev and Sandler (2019).

or failing states, or states experiencing war, are more likely arenas for terrorists' activity, these factors alone are insufficient for explaining terrorism (Coggins, 2015). Scholars find the most significant contributor to terrorist affiliation to be a lack of civil liberties, rather than specific qualities of any given region, demographic area, race, or ethnicity (Hassan, 2001; Krueger and Malečková, 2003; Lee, 2011).

A country's political freedom and history of political transitions can help explain its experience with terrorism (Abadie, 2006). Poor institutional environments effectively lower the opportunity cost of engaging in terrorism, as individuals have few ways to peaceably voice discontent or participate in markets to improve their conditions in a scalable way. Embedded in these institutional inadequacies is the fundamental failing to protect property rights, such protection being necessary for robust markets. A healthy domestic economy not only lowers the risk of ethnic violence but significantly lessens the chance of ethnic tension culminating in transnational terrorism (Basuchoudhary and Shughart, 2010). Ethnic fractionalization and distinctions are ubiquitous, but violent conflict is not (Fearon and Laitin, 1996). Understanding these institutional constraints is integral to making sense of seemingly "irrational outcomes" – willing involvement in violent activity, suicide bombing, and so on – under the rational actor model.

This Element draws on insights from Austrian economics and public choice economics to understand both the contextual and the emergent nature of terrorism with a view to informing policy and statecraft in fighting terrorism. Applying these insights is important for understanding the complex global network of terrorism, the economic foundations for such behavior, and the persistence of terrorist organizations despite worldwide efforts to detain and punish perpetrators of terrorism.

Consensus on a universal definition of terrorism is lacking (see Schmid, 1983; Weinberg, Pedahzur, and Hirsch-Hoefler, 2004; Lutz and Lutz, 2005: 6). The post-9/11 increase in terrorism-related scholarship has done nothing to alleviate this lack of agreement. Particular hurdles to a universal definition include legal considerations, the tendency to conflate terrorism with other forms of political behavior (see Rathbone and Rowley, 2002), and subjective value judgments about behavior (e.g., one person's "terrorist" is another person's "freedom fighter") (see Kennedy, 1999; Ganor, 2002; Sageman, 2008; Shughart, 2011).

We employ the definition of terrorism generally adopted by US government agencies. The Department of Defense (DOD) defines terrorism as "the unlawful use of violence or threat of violence, often motivated by religious, political, or other ideological beliefs, to instill fear and coerce governments or societies in pursuit of goals that are usually political" (Joint Chiefs of Staff, 2014: vii). We use this characterization of terrorism for three reasons.

First, this definition captures the essential elements of what is generally accepted as terrorism: (1) the unlawful use of force, (2) activities conducted for the purpose of instilling fear beyond the terrorist event, and (3) activities undertaken with the goal of instituting political change. Importantly, this definition separates "terrorism" from violent and suppressive activities committed by states; that kind of "state-sponsored terrorism" is outside the scope of this Element. Second, this definition aligns well with what the literature has identified as the purpose of terrorist activities. Terrorists look to create psychological repercussions that extend beyond the attack and target (Crenshaw, 1995; Hoffman, 2017: 43; Ackerman et al., 2006). This definition illustrates that terrorism is purposive action on the part of terrorist actors. It is a means to an end – intended to induce some form of change – political or otherwise. This is important as terrorism is yet another form of purposive human action; this places terror activity in the analytical domain of political economy. Third, this definition allows us to better analyze counterterrorism policy, using the government's own definition. We will be better able to ascertain whether counterterrorism policy is obtaining its desired results and if not, what can be done differently.

We proceed as follows. Section 2 provides a discussion of the foundations of the economics of terrorism, emphasizing that terrorist behavior is purposeful and goal-oriented, that all of the decision-making processes of terrorists and terrorist organizations entail subjective evaluation of costs and benefits, and that the terrorist market, like all others, consists of suppliers and demanders. From this perspective, terrorism is a phenomenon that can be traced to the individual choices of people embedded in a complex set of institutions.

In Section 3 we turn to counterterrorism policy. We consider three categories of policies – income-based policies, price-based policies, and opportunity cost–based policies – and discuss the economics of each. We then discuss the importance of institutions for counterterrorism policy. Institutions matter because without changes to the deeper environment that incentivizes terrorism, the root cause will persist. Income- and price-based policies might reduce terrorism in a particular time and place, but, absent other changes, these policies will not reduce the underlying demand for terrorism itself. Given this, we then discuss the implications for institutional change and the feasibility of such efforts.

Section 4 considers three dilemmas facing liberal societies related to counterterrorism efforts: the vulnerability of liberal societies to terrorism, the potential erosion of liberal values in general, and the possible permanent expansion of government and loss of domestic liberties. To engage in this discussion, we present two alternative models of government growth. The first, the trade-off model, views liberty and security as a trade-off balanced by a well-functioning democratic government that seeks to maximize the welfare of its citizens. The second, the ratchet effect model, offers insight into how government can permanently grow (in scale and scope) in the face of a crisis. We discuss the pathologies of democratic decision-making and how these frictions can influence counterterrorism policy.

Section 5 provides an assessment of the US government's war on terror, which turned twenty years old in 2021. We discuss the origins of the war, whether it can be judged a success or a failure (relative to the baseline set by those who initiated it), and some of the main effects abroad and within the United States. Section 6 concludes by putting forward several areas for future research.

## 2 The Economic Foundations of Terrorism

### Purposive Plans and Actions

Terrorism is an emergent phenomenon; it arises from the culmination of calculated choices, and those choices can change. Terrorists and aspiring terrorists act after they assess the likely outcomes of their plans; as such, terrorism falls within the category of rational choice. Societies plagued by high or increasing levels of terrorism represent an emergent order of violent competition and plunder rather than the peaceful cooperation facilitated by the market order. Terrorists are goal-oriented (Shughart, 2011) and their plans are "calculated and systematic" (Hoffman, 1998: 15). This is consistent with Mises (1998) who noted that people act purposefully to achieve their goals. Just as we would state that a businessman acts to generate profit or a politician acts purposefully to win reelection, we can say the same for a terrorist. A terrorist acts to obtain some end.

Terrorists face resource constraints in terms of the budgets, time, and knowledge available to them. They must choose how, when, and where to allocate their scarce resources (Shughart, 2011). Each choice carries with it an opportunity cost – or the next best alternative that must be forgone. For example, the decision to dedicate time and human capital to carrying out a specific attack means fewer resources available for alternative plans. Terrorists choose to allocate their time and capital across an array of activities, both legal and illegal, violent and nonviolent. The ultimate mix of activities selected will be based on their own subjective perceptions of the relative costs and benefits of each activity. As we would expect any other economic actor to change their behavior when circumstances change, so the terrorist will adjust to changing costs and constraints. Policies can make things temporarily more costly for terrorists, but if the underlying issues that cause people to demand terrorism – that is, the contextual environment and the terrorists' perceptions of the rules and constraints – do not change, we will forever be fighting and creating the unintended consequence of more, rather than less, terrorists and terrorism.

Some post-9/11 scholarship on terrorism has attempted to ascertain whether terrorists have a "type" – that is, universal or common attributes that explain who becomes a terrorist and why. These attempts to typify a terrorist have been largely unsuccessful; not poverty, race, religion, employment, or social status alone can create a terrorist profile (Laqueur, 1999; Pape, 2005; Shughart, 2011). The motivation behind uncovering some single "profile" is rooted in policy. If authorities could identify would-be terrorists prior to their actions, they could implement policies to stop them. But such an understanding of terrorism fails to appreciate the underlying economic problem facing terrorists and potential terrorists. Terrorists are not some monolithic group; rather, they are individuals who assess their environments and act based on their own subjective valuations. Changing the costs and benefits faced by terrorists will alter their behavior, but effectively changing incentives surrounding possible terrorists is no simple matter.

The modern terrorism of al-Qaeda, Islamic State in Iraq and Syria (ISIS), Hamas, and others is illustrative. Each group, through its various activities, uses violence and other means in an effort to achieve particular ends. To understand al-Qaeda, for example, we must apply the logic of human action to the individual actors within the organization and see al-Qaeda as an emergent phenomenon, part of the "third wave" of post-World War II terrorism (Shughart, 2011). This includes attempting to understand the conditions influencing the perceived costs and benefits facing specific terrorists, and the organizations to which they belong. As conditions and perceptions change, so too do the costs and benefits as perceived by terrorists.

To provide an example of evolving conditions, consider that the third wave of modern terrorism is tied to the Iranian Revolution of 1979 (Enders and Sandler, 2000). This wave of terrorism was exacerbated by the collapse of the Soviet Union in the early 1990s and a decade of fighting against the Mujahideen in Central Asia (Shughart, 2011: 6). Those specific political conditions contributed to the formation of the terrorism we see today, which continues to morph and adapt.

Osama bin Laden, the founder and cult personality within al-Qaeda, clearly stated his grievances about American intervention in the Middle East, and how Saudi Arabia was the impetus for al-Qaeda's emergence. In a 1996 interview, bin Laden stated:

The ordinary man knows that [Saudi Arabia] is the largest oil producer in the world, yet at the same time he is suffering from taxes and bad services. Now the people understand the speeches of the ulemas in the mosques – that our country has become an American colony. They act decisively with every action to kick the Americans out of Saudi Arabia. What happened in Riyadh and [Dhahran] when 24 Americans were killed in two bombings is clear evidence of the huge anger of Saudi people against America. The Saudis now know their real enemy is America. (quoted in Foreign Broadcast Information Service, 2004: 12)

The Taliban emerged in 1994 in Afghanistan in response to the Soviet invasion and imposed an authoritarian Islamic state over three-quarters of Afghanistan until 2001 (Katzman and Thomas, 2017). After the US withdrawal from Afghanistan in 2021, the Taliban regained control of the country. In addition to the Taliban, the most prolific terror groups today – ISIS/Islamic State of Iraq and the Levant (ISIL),[3] Boko Haram, and al-Shabaab (Institute for Economics and Peace, 2020: 15) – all fall under this third wave of post-World War II terrorism. As conditions change, we should expect terrorism to change, in both the organizing principles of the groups and the tactics they use.

Even the most ruthless terrorist groups, such as IS, respond to incentives. In its early days, IS was quite successful as a terrorist group; it was able to drive Iraqi security forces out of key cities and to capture the city of Mosul in Iraq (Al-Salhy and Arango, 2014). It pursued ostentatious and brutal tactics, including releasing videos of beheadings and executions.

At one time IS had 30,000 fighters, an annual budget of a billion dollars (Fawaz, 2016), and the support of military affiliates in 12 countries (Zavadski, 2014). As a point of comparison, consider that at the time of the 9/11 attacks (estimated to cost a mere $500,000) al-Qaeda had a budget of 30 million dollars per year financed through Islamic charities and donors (Roth, Greenburg, and Wille, n.d.). Yet no matter its financial prowess or its military manpower, IS was damaged by forces that fought against it in 2014 under Operation Inherent Resolve, killing thousands of its troops and reducing its financial strength (*Straits Times*, 2017). The costs rose, the targets hardened, and ISIL lost key territories, which forced members to retreat and redirect their efforts.

Policymakers considered the fight against ISIL to be a success. However, what did not change were the underlying conditions that made joining ISIL attractive in the first place. Terrorism is an effort to obtain social change. As such, we must assess why terrorism is an attractive option relative to

---

[3] The names ISIS and ISIL are used somewhat interchangeably but the group has called itself Islamic State (IS) since 2014 when it declared itself a global caliphate. It is an Islamist jihadist militant group that subscribes to a Salafi jihadist doctrine within Sunni Islam. It was founded in 1999 and pledged its allegiance to al-Qaeda.

alternatives. This matters for the way we think about the efficacy of counter-terrorism policies in both the short term and the long term.

## Supply of and Demand for Terrorism

Terrorism is about the use of violence and fear to engender political change. For most people living in societies with economic, human, and political freedom, the cost of engaging in terrorism is high relative to the expected payoffs. In cases where economic, political, and other forms of freedom are weak or absent, terrorism is more likely to emerge because the opportunity cost of engaging in terrorist activities is comparatively lower.

Terrorists can act independently – that is, be "lone-wolf" terrorists (see Kenyon, Baker-Beall, and Binder, 2021) – or as part of a group. Terrorists and terrorist organizations can be understood through the lens of economics. Like all human actors, the terrorist must weigh the expected benefit against the expected costs of group membership. The leadership must make similar calculations when forming the group. The challenge for the terrorist organization is like the challenges facing other organizations, which entail aligning the incentives of the participants and the leadership in the pursuit of the organization's overarching mission. The rewards and internal incentives for terrorist members must be aligned with the overall goals of the organization for the group to be successful.

We can conceptualize terrorism as we could any other economic good – being both demanded by hypothetical consumers and produced by hypothetical suppliers. From the consumer side, we consider a consumer's willingness and ability to pay for terrorism relative to other alternative goods. The higher the price of terrorism, the less terrorism is consumed by potential "buyers." Just as conditions in the market for butter or automobiles change the overarching demand for butter and automobiles, changing conditions alter the demand for terrorism. Changes in preferences or ideology, expectations about the future, income, the price of complementary or substitute goods will all change the demand for terrorism. To the extent that terrorists provide collective or public goods to their members and beyond, terrorism solves collective action problems within societies (Oberschall, 2006), which will contribute to the demand for the activities of the terrorist organization.

Terrorists on the supply side organize into nonprofit, paramilitary organizations, or act as proto-states. They operate like a nonprofit bureau in which they raise their own revenues through legal and illegal means and through donor contributions. To provide an example, in a post-9/11 raid in Bosnia, authorities discovered documents related to what members of al-Qaeda referred to as the

"Golden Chain." This included a list of twenty elite Saudi businessmen, bankers, and former ministers and charities who were the early funders of Osama bin Laden (Simpson, 2003). The list dates to the early days of al-Qaeda during the Soviet invasion of Afghanistan in which money was given to bin Laden who used it to carry out his jihadist movement and later fund al-Qaeda, and in some cases funneled through charities and nongovernmental organizations (Prados and Blanchard, 2004; National Commission on Terrorist Attacks, 2004: 55). The goals and tactics of terrorist groups often change, as did al-Qaeda's, and now ISIL's in the face of military defeat, but the key to reducing the supply of terrorism is understanding and addressing the demand for terrorism. Terrorist sympathizers are both financially contributing to the organization (the supply) and willing and able to "pay" for what the organization does (the demand).

Terrorist organizations produce services with public good characteristics (Shughart, 2011) as the benefits are shared by all who favor the terrorists' activities (Rathbone and Rowley, 2002); thus, they face free-rider problems. To overcome these potential free-riding issues, terrorist organizations often offer "selective incentives" – incentives that create private benefits for activities with public characteristics, incentivizing active participation by members who otherwise engage in free riding off the efforts of others (Olson, 1965; Lichbach, 1994, 1996). For example, the expected payoff for members can take the form of financial rewards, status, group membership, appointment to public office if the group seizes political power, access to education, job training, or social services otherwise unavailable (Zakaria, 2003: 142). Similarly, terrorists supply social welfare benefits (Zakaria, 2003; Berman and Iannaccone, 2006; Shughart, 2011) to members and, in the cases of suicide terrorism, to the members' families.

For selective incentives to be effective, organizations must develop effective mechanisms to sort people into groups – contributors and noncontributors – in order to reward participation and punish nonparticipation. Group size and the number of people to coordinate are key factors in the efficacy of selective incentives. Hammond and Axelrod (2006) argue that ethnocentrism helps sort out free riders. Strong religious ties within the group or within cells of the group may have similar sorting power within the terrorist organization, leading to greater organizational efficacy and reducing the chances of individual defection. This might explain why many terrorist organizations limit group membership and why they are often organizationally compartmentalized into small "cells" to reduce internal monitoring costs (Shughart, 2011: 20). This also potentially insulates the group from external infiltration from law enforcement or counterterrorism agencies.

## Terrorists and Counterterrorists: Two Peas in a Methodological Pod

The same foundational principles that apply to terrorists apply to those engaged in counterterrorism. The goals are different – terrorists want to perpetuate terror while counterterrorists want to prevent terrorism – but the underlying principles are the same. Those designing counterterrorism policy act purposefully to achieve their desired goals. They face opportunity costs in deciding to pursue one course of action over another.

Counterterrorism policy is not formulated in a vacuum. It emerges from an array of institutions – formal and informal. As Coyne (2015, 2020a) emphasizes, there is no "defense brain," meaning that it is not sufficient to treat "the state" as an all-knowing supercomputer that simply produces security policies that maximize the welfare of the domestic populace. Instead, security policy emerges through a supply and demand process through time. The institutions within which counterterrorists are embedded will influence the types of policies that emerge. As with the economic analysis of public economics in general (Buchanan, 1949), the analysis of counterterrorism policy requires appreciating that actors pursue their goals within a certain institutional structure that influences how they perceive the costs and benefits of alternative courses of action.

Moreover, there are interaction effects. The behavior of terrorists will influence the counterterrorism market and vice versa. Other interaction effects can be observed between governments in charge of counterterrorism policy and the domestic populaces they serve. Counterterrorism policy is not neutral with respect to the fabric of domestic life. Counterterrorism policies can, and do, change domestic institutions and, therefore, the payoffs facing people who live within those institutions.

## Summing Up

Terrorism is about choices made by individuals pursuing specific plans. In making these choices, people weigh the costs and benefits based on their perceptions of the world. People are embedded in an array of institutions – formal and informal – and this will, in conjunction with their own expectations about the future, influence the perceived payoffs to different potential actions. The market for terrorism, like any other market, consists of suppliers and demanders. Perceived value and cost (i.e., opportunity cost) are subjective for people on both sides of the market. Further, actors must navigate an array of challenges, including uncertainty, collective action problems in group formation and operation, and changing local and global conditions.

The same framework can be used to understand counterterrorism policy. The goals of counterterrorism are different from those of terrorists, but the analytical framework for understanding the decision-making process is the same. From this perspective, the variation in outcomes can be understood through focusing on the institutional contexts, rather than on agent type (e.g., "rational" or "irrational," "good" or "bad").

Given this economic foundation for understanding terrorists and terrorist organizations, we now turn to a more careful consideration of counterterrorism. We consider three types of counterterrorism policies followed by a discussion of the importance of institutions, and institutional change, for the desire to reduce terrorism.

## 3 Counterterrorism

## Economics of Counterterrorism

Counterterrorism refers to government activities to prevent terrorist attacks or to limit their impact. There are three main categories of counterterrorism policies: (1) income-based policies, (2) price-based policies, and (3) opportunity cost–based policies. Within each of the categories, activities can be offensive or defensive (Enders and Sandler, 2012: 103–125). Offensive activities seek to directly and proactively engage terrorists. Defense activities aim to raise the cost of (i.e., defend against) future terrorist acts without directly engaging a specific person or group. Let us consider each of the three policy categories in turn.

### Income-Based Policies

Income-based policies seek to reduce the resources available to terrorist groups. Effective income-based policies will reduce the resources available to terrorists (i.e., shift the terrorist's budget line inward) and, thus, restrict the activities they can afford. Offensive income-based policies would entail directly confiscating the resources of a specific person or group deemed to be a terrorist. For instance, in 2020 the US government seized 300 cryptocurrency accounts, worth the equivalent of two million dollars, alleging that these accounts were being used to fund the operations of al-Qaeda, Hamas, and IS (Savage, 2020). Defensive income-based policies are broader and aim to discourage future terrorist activities. For example, the USA PATRIOT Act broadened the powers of the US government to combat money laundering, including such activities that may provide financial assets to terrorist organizations. Making it more difficult to hide financial assets forces would-be terrorists to go to additional efforts to cover their financial tracks. This raises the costs of engaging in terrorist activities, thereby reducing the number of activities that can be pursued. In many cases policy tools can potentially be used in both offensive and defensive ways. The PATRIOT Act, for instance, can be used to target specific people or specific groups (offensive), but it also has a defensive component since it raises the cost of future terrorist activities and, therefore, might disincentivize certain behaviors beyond any preidentified group.

Income-based policies can be effective where the behavior of terrorist groups is sensitive to the quantity of resources available. This requires that alternative sources of income are limited. If other sources of income are available, the terrorist organization may simply fill the gap created by income-based policies by substituting toward other income sources. Likewise, if terrorist activities are not highly dependent on resources available, then income-based policies are likely to be limited in their effectiveness.

### Price-Based Policies

Price-based policies seek to create a disincentive to engage in terrorism by raising the relative price of certain behaviors. Price changes (graphically represented by the rotation of the budget line facing terrorists) mean that one activity becomes more expensive relative to other activities (the price of other activities held constant). An example of an offensive price-based policy would be government efforts to infiltrate terrorist organizations for information-gathering purposes. If terrorists are aware of this possibility, they may adjust their behavior and the activities of their organization. An example of a defensive price-based policy would entail "hardening" specific targets against potential attack. This might include establishing new security technologies or procedures in order to raise the cost of terrorist activities. In an early paper on the economics of terrorism, Landes (1978) found that installation of metal detectors at airports reduced the number of skyjackings. The underlying logic is that the metal detectors raised the relative price of terrorists engaging in airplane hijackings because it was harder to bring metal weapons onboard due to the increased likelihood of detection.

### Income Effects and Substitution Effects of Income- and Price-Based Policies, and Entrepreneurial Terrorists

Economic treatments of counterterrorism policy emphasize income and substitution effects, which refers to changes in behavior due to changes in the budget constraint (income-based policies) or in relative prices (price-based policies) (Enders and Sandler, 2004; Anderton and Carter, 2005, 2006). The logic of the income effect is as follows. Effective income-based policies reduce the resources available to terrorists. This incentivizes terrorists to change their behavior by reallocating their efforts from those activities that require more resources (are more expensive) to those activities that require fewer (are less expensive). Terrorist actions requiring more resources that may have been feasible under the original budget constraint are no longer feasible under the new, post-counterterrorism budget constraint. Terrorists will adjust their behavior accordingly by either changing their action to that which is affordable or redirecting some of their time to seeking out new sources of funding to increase their budget. Changes in behavior can be changes in organizational structure or focus or changes in how a given organization carries out its operations.

Substitution effects occur as people adjust their behavior due to relative price changes. In the context of terrorism, effective price-based counterterrorism policies raise the relative price of engaging in certain activities. At the same time, they reduce the price of engaging in other activities. For example, effectively hardening certain potential targets raises the price of attacking those specific targets. All else constant, this will reduce terrorist attacks against those targets. At the same time, however, the relative prices of attacking other, "softer" targets fall. This makes it more likely that these softer targets will come under attack. Stated more broadly, terrorists respond to the price changes created by counterterrorism policies by substituting into other, lower-priced terrorist activities.

The income and substitution effects related to counterterrorism policy can be domestic or international. For example, a government might make airports more secure, which raises the cost of terrorists carrying out aircraft-based terrorist acts. But this might cause terrorists to substitute by attacking other domestic targets that are relatively cheaper compared to the hardened airport target. Alternatively, terrorists might substitute their efforts toward international targets. For instance, a government might protect its domestic assets, which makes its foreign assets a more likely terrorist target (holding the protection of those foreign assets constant). At a national level, new and effective domestic counterterrorism policies by one country may make other countries less safe (all else constant) as terrorists redirect their activities to other countries in response to the price change.

Also relevant is the Alchian–Allen effect, or the third law of demand (Alchian and Allen, 1983). This holds that when the price of two substitute goods – for example, high- and low-quality products – are both increased by a fixed per-unit amount, consumption will shift toward the higher-quality product. This is because the addition of the fixed per-unit amount decreases the relative price of the higher-quality good. In the context of terrorism, the different qualities of goods, from the perspective of the terrorist, refer to more-deadly methods (higher quality) and less-deadly methods (lower quality) and the fixed cost refers to counterterrorism policies – for example, the cost of avoidance, the associated punishments if caught, or the expectation of being labeled a terrorist and incurring the associated costs. In this case terrorists substitute toward more-deadly methods as they become relative cheaper. An increase in the expectations terrorists have of the punishment they will receive if caught, or overuse or expansion of the label "terrorism" itself, could encourage increased violence, per this logic.

The main takeaway is that counterterrorism policies often do not eradicate terrorism but instead change the composition of terrorist activities. Counterterrorism policies are best understood as an action–reaction process between governments and (current and potential) terrorists. Terrorists are perceived as posing an imminent or future threat. This threat results in a counterterrorism response by government with the aim of reducing the resources available to terrorists (income-based policy) or raising the price of certain acts (price-based policy). Terrorists respond to the change in income or relative price by substituting into other activities. Government must then decide whether to react with new counterterrorism policy – and the back-and-forth continues.

In responding to counterterrorism policies, terrorists act entrepreneurially, which can frustrate government efforts. As an example, consider the effects of the Afghan and Iraq insurgencies substituting into improvised explosive devices (IEDs) during the US government's occupation. In his analysis of IEDs, Wood (2018) notes that US military occupiers were at first unprepared for IEDs and relied on attaching makeshift armor (e.g., scrap metal) to their vehicles for protection. To fill this gap, the US government spent billions of dollars on creating and updating technologies and techniques to counter IEDs. In response to these policy changes by the US government, the insurgents adjusted their methods and techniques for deploying IEDs. In many instances, the insurgents adopted more rudimentary forms of IEDs – simple explosives with basic detonators – to make the US government's technology irrelevant. The result was that, despite the massive investment by the US government, IED incidents grew over a period during the occupations (see Cordesman, Loi, and Kocharlakota, 2010). This was because IEDs themselves are relatively cheap to alter but the policies required to thwart them are relatively expensive. Having such a policy does not lower the output of the terrorist organization but rather creates the unintended consequence of increasing the use of IEDs.

As this illustrates, counterterrorism polices result in adaptation by entrepreneurially alert actors. Although economists typically discuss entrepreneurial alertness in the context of markets, with particular focus on resource (re) allocation through arbitrage and innovation (see Kirzner, 1973, 1997), a similar logic can be applied to terrorists who attempt to efficiently allocate resources and innovate to meet their goals, leading to superfluous discovery as a direct result of the interventions (Kirzner 1985). Scholars working in the Austrian tradition have discussed the role of entrepreneurship in a variety of nonmarket settings (see Boettke and Prychitko, 2004; Chamlee-Wright and Myers, 2008; Chamlee-Wright, 2010; Storr, Haeffele-Balch, and Grube, 2015, 2017; Aligica, 2015, 2018; Boettke, 2018; Aligica, Boettke, and Tarko, 2019). This scholarship focuses on issues of alertness to opportunities, feedback, and the process of coordination and adjustment in the absence of competitive prices and profit and loss. A similar logic could be applied to terrorist organizations.

## Opportunity Cost–Based Policies

The third category of counterterrorism policies focuses on changing the opportunity cost facing (actual or potential) terrorists. Opportunity cost refers to the anticipated value placed on the next best alternative that is rejected when making a choice. It is the expected value forgone when making a choice. When someone chooses to engage in terrorist activities, they are necessarily giving up some other value that they could have obtained if they had chosen the next best alternative. The idea behind opportunity cost–based counterterrorism policies is as follows.

If government policy can effectively raise the opportunity cost of engaging in terrorism then, on the margin (and holding all else constant), fewer people will engage in terrorist acts because the alternative to terrorism will be more attractive. Effective policies in this category may redirect current terrorists while discouraging future terrorists as well. One example of this category of policies are efforts to foster economic development. The underlying idea is that if there are more economic opportunities available from nonterrorist activities, people will be less likely to engage in terrorism because the cost of doing so – in terms of forgone income – has increased.

This logic was at the core of the US government's aid strategy in Afghanistan, which was aimed at winning the "hearts and minds" of Afghan citizens (see Fishstein and Wilder, 2012). The idea was that well-spent humanitarian and development aid could create a secure environment that is conducive to economic development. These benefits would raise the cost of supporting insurgent and terrorist groups, which would undermine the legitimacy and sustainability of these groups while reinforcing the US government's vision of reconstructed Afghan institutions. However, because there is no "defense brain" from which we can cull an omniscient set of policies, these efforts can have the disastrous unintended consequence of keeping poor nations poor and further exacerbating the incentives for the use of terrorism. If policymakers, in their efforts to stop terrorism, freeze the wrong assets, use a drone on civilians, or create an inhospitable environment for investment and trade, those policies could foster more terrorism.

## Summing Up

The three categories of counterterrorism policy are not mutually exclusive; in practice, governments often adopt a mix of proactive and defensive strategies and a blend of income-based, price-based, and opportunity cost–based policies. Given the possible counterterrorism strategy types, a crucial issue is the formation and implementation of policy. Terrorism policy is produced through a political process, and a complete consideration of counterterrorism policy must take this into account. Epistemic constraints and the particular incentives facing policymakers will influence the types of policies selected and how they are implemented. We explore the specifics of this process in Section 4 when discussing models of state security provision.

Another issue is the possibility of negative unintended consequences associated with counterterrorism policy. Income- and price-based policies rely on deterrence – that is, a "stick" rather than a "carrot" – to attempt to induce change in terrorist behavior. However, counterintuitively, this emphasis might strengthen the demand for terrorism. As Frey (2004: 33–36) notes, focus on deterrence policies contributes to a negative-sum situation between terrorists and terrorism-combating governments. It can create, and entrench, a situation where coercive action is met with coercive action, which can spiral into an ongoing process of negative-sum violence.

A key part of counterterrorism is appreciating the underlying institutional conditions that create the demand for terrorist activities. An effective income- or price-based policy might reduce certain types or quantities of terrorist activities in the immediate term. However, without deeper institutional changes the factors contributing to the demand for terrorism as a perceived mechanism of social change will persist. Combating this requires an appreciation of the institutional context within which terrorists and terrorist organizations emerge and operate.

## Importance of Institutions and Institutional Change

Institutions matter in determining individuals' perceptions and the personal choices they make or abstain from making. Mises (1998: 46) suggests the importance of "inheritance and environment for man's actions ... He lives not simply as man *in abstracto*, he lives as a son of his family, his people, and his age … His ideology is what his environment enjoins upon him." Man is not impotent here; man "is ready to change his ideology and consequently his mode of action whenever he becomes convinced that this would better serve his own interests" (Mises 1988: 46). Boettke and Storr (2002: 170) explain that "social phenomena, social structures, social relationships and social actions are unintelligible without considering how actors subjectively perceive them." What these authors emphasize is that people are not self-contained or isolated individuals; rather, they exist in society and that social existence determines how they assess expected benefits against expected costs. Terrorists are no different.

The previously discussed third wave of terrorism exists largely within the context of religious radicalism, particularly radical Islam. While there is no universal terrorist "type," there are institutional factors that make terrorism attractive as a mechanism of social change. It would be an overstatement to suggest that radical Islamic terrorism is only religious in nature. Already there are nearly 2 billion Muslims in the world, and this number is expected to climb to more than 2.2 billion by 2030 (see Fustos, 2011). At the same time, terrorism represents a small portion of overall human activity. In 2017, terrorism accounted for 0.05 percent of all deaths, a drop from its early 2000s peak of 0.08 percent (Ritchie et al., 2019: n.p.). If modern terrorism were strictly a problem of religion or religious extremism, we would expect more of it (Caplan, 2006). This suggests that we must examine terrorism in the broader context of the institutional environment in which terrorists live and thrive.

We conceptualize the relationship between the three main institutional spheres as illustrated in Figure 1. It is significant that the spheres overlap but are not one and the same; thus, there is competition for resource allocation and problem solving. Boundaries in the arenas of social life create important incentives for how and where problems are solved. As those spheres become less distinct, the stakes for controlling social outcomes – religious rules and norms, law, economic affairs, and political decision-making – are higher. This leads to a single authoritarian power structure in which the decentralized mechanisms and incentives for problem solving and cooperation are destroyed. Society becomes a winner-take-all game and the incentives for peaceful cooperation diminish.

In markets, resources are allocated privately through the market process, which is grounded in property rights, prices, and profits and losses. Markets adjudicate the allocation of scarce resources through the productive incentives of private entrepreneurship in the quest for profit (Kirzner, 1973, 2000). This creates incentives for firms and suppliers to discover new and better ways to create value for as many people as possible. Knowledge is decentralized and exists in local form (Hayek, 1945); thus, decentralized market prices bring together the

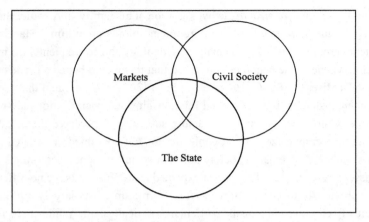

**Figure 1** Institutional spheres of society

**Source:** Created by the authors.

most willing suppliers and consumers through the ongoing process of commercial exchange. Markets create abundance over time through specialization and growing productivity as well as social trust through voluntary cooperation.

Alternatively, the state has monopoly on coercion and uses directives through policy and bureaucracy to allocate scarce resources without the very mechanisms that make markets work well – private property rights, market prices, and profits and losses. Moreover, when the state expends resources over a range of projects, it necessarily means that those resources are not available for alternative uses – that is, state resources have opportunity costs. This means that the state experiencing growth in its sphere crowds out activity in the other sectors because the state must pull resources out of those other sectors to engage them in its projects. When the state takes over resource allocation of any kind, therefore, winners and losers emerge (Wagner, 2017).

Even in the most well-functioning societies where the government largely respects the rule of law and strives for political liberalism, the government creates allocative inefficiencies, is unable to assess value creation, lacks appropriate corrective mechanisms and the ability to adjust quickly to changing circumstances, and is subject to special interests and the desire for certain groups to obtain power and the associated political rents. In the worst-performing societies, where robust markets do not guide resource allocation through the price mechanism and profits and losses, peaceful, positive-sum cooperation is not a repeated game.

The third sphere represents civil society. Civil society is the space where people volunteer, live in families, and associate with neighbors and community members, and where philanthropic activity emerges. Like markets, civil society operates on the voluntary principle of association; the difference is that civil society, unlike markets, does not rely on competitive prices and profits and losses to allocate scarce resources. A robust civil society is essential for a thriving market and serves as an important constraint upon the inherent tendencies of the state to grow in both size and scope (Tocqueville, 1969).

Today, terrorism thrives in societies with weak, exclusive, and extractive institutions and where the spheres of markets and civil society are limited or crowded out by all-encompassing authoritarian states or alien occupiers. In these societies, mechanisms for cooperative social change and for the peaceful mitigation of disputes are limited. The institutional framework for cooperative and peaceful problem solving is lacking and incentives for terrorist violence become more attractive alternatives. To illustrate this, consider Table 1, which compares the ten countries with the most terrorism activity, attacks, and deaths, listed in order from Afghanistan (Institute for Economics and Peace, 2020), against several indicators of human progress and well-being, namely, political freedom, economic freedom, human freedom, gross domestic profit (GDP) per capita, and the World Bank's Ease of Doing Business Index.

Taken together, these metrics give us some sense of the institutions in each country and whether they are inclusive, liberal, and cooperative, or more exclusive and extractive.

Societies that score relatively high on these indicators are societies that foster trust and cooperation, which provide nonviolent mechanisms for dispute resolution and social change. Greater economic freedom reduces the number of terrorist attacks in ethnically tense societies (Basuchdoudhary and Shughart, 2010). Greater political freedom combined with greater economic freedom also fosters community and civic participation, which contributes to trust among strangers and provides vehicles for nonviolent dispute resolution. Human freedom measures personal, economic, and civil freedoms such as gender equality, social mobility, religious freedom, freedom of association, and freedom of expression (Vásquez and McMahon, 2020).

A lack of voluntary associations and civic institutions that allow for peaceful arbitrage and cooperative solutions along with a weak or nonexistent rule of law are the very things that foster terrorism as a mechanism for social change. The Institute for Economics and Peace (2020: 5) reports that "high levels of group grievance and low levels of the rule of law are correlated with terrorism across all countries." Take Afghanistan, for example. The country is riddled with political, economic, and social problems and the battles for control permeate all spheres of life and culture. Afghanistan is dominated by sectarian strife where the political elite is a source of plunder and exploitation.

**Table 1** Countries with the highest level of terrorist activity and their institutions

| Countries most affected by terrorism | Global Terrorism Index[4] | Economic Freedom Index | Human Freedom Index | GDP per capita (2020) (constant USD, 2015) | Ease of Doing Business Index |
|---|---|---|---|---|---|
| Afghanistan | 9.9592 | — | — | $529.70 | 44.1 |
| Iraq | 8.682 | 5.61 | 4.9 | $4,247.80 | 44.7 |
| Nigeria | 8.314 | 6.93 | 6.05 | $2,396.00 | 56.9 |
| Syria | 7.778 | 5.45 | 3.97 | $952.90[5] | 42.0 |
| Somalia | 7.645 | — | — | $444.80 | 20.0 |
| Yemen | 7.581 | 5.51 | 4.17 | $1,290.90[6] | 31.8 |
| Pakistan | 7.541 | 6.07 | 5.64 | $1,446.80 | 61.0 |
| India | 7.353 | 6.56 | 6.43 | $1,811.70 | 71.0 |
| Democratic Republic of Congo | 7.178 | 5.15 | 5.29 | $505.30 | 36.2 |
| Philippines | 7.099 | 7.43 | 6.9 | $3,269.70 | 62.8 |

---

[4] The Global Terrorism Index ranges from 1 to 10 with 10 the worst; the Economic Freedom Index and the Human Freedom Index range from 0 to 10 with 10 the best; the Ease of Doing Business Index ranges from 1 to 100 with 100 the best. Table created by authors. Sources of data: Global Terrorism Index, see Institute for Economics and Peace, 2020; Economic Freedom Index and Human Freedom Index, see Vásquez and McMahon, 2020; GDP data, see World Bank, 2022; Ease of Doing Business Index, see World Bank, 2020.

[5] Data for Syria are from 2019, the most recent year available.

[6] Data for Yemen are from 2018, the most recent year available.

Five out of the top ten terrorist countries – Afghanistan, Iraq, Syria, Yemen, and Somalia – are in a state of war (Institute for Economics and Peace, 2020). Moreover, Yemen, Iraq, and Afghanistan are ruled by authoritarian theocracies. They do not have robust economic or civic institutions for conflict resolution and promoting the harmonious coexistence of different groups, tribes, sects, and so on. The battle for control is fierce; it is a winner-take-all game. Terrorists have a greater incentive to act in such societies as opposed to those with institutions that foster cooperation.

## Summing Up: Implications for Counterterrorism

Terrorists change their targets, techniques, and locations in an effort to avoid being caught. If we want a permanent reduction in terrorism, however, it is not enough simply to harden targets or launch military offensives, such as Operation Inherent Resolve that pushed back IS in Iraq and Syria, and expect that this will make the terrorists stop altogether what they are doing. It will only cause them to change their behavior, substitute into doing other things, and move their base of operations to more favorable conditions. For example, in 2019, IS continued to decline in the Middle East and North Africa, but in sub-Saharan Africa, IS-affiliated groups increased their activity. As this suggests, terrorist organizations substitute into other tactics and targets while making new partnerships that often cause terrorism to spread to new regions.

Less terrorism requires greater economic, political, civil, and social freedoms. The societal conditions in which terrorism emerges foster the demand for terrorist activity as a mechanism for social change. Supply is a response to perceived demand; reducing the demand for terrorism requires institutional reform in the direction of economic, political, and human freedoms that foster greater trust and provide an environment for peaceful problem solving. The question then becomes the source of this institutional change. Drawing upon a range of concepts and insights from the Austrian tradition, existing scholarship studies the limitations of foreign intervention and efforts to engage in nation-building and economic development (Coyne, 2008, 2013; Coyne and Boettke, 2009; Coyne and Mathers, 2010; Coyne and Pellillo, 2011; Duncan and Coyne, 2015; Henderson, 2016; Murtazashvili, 2016; Coyne and Bradley, 2019; Murtazashvili and Murtazashvili, 2019, 2020, 2021). Pape (2005) contends that foreign military occupation is a driving causal factor behind terrorist attacks. Taken together, this literature calls into question the feasibility of exogenous institutional change for reducing terrorism both in the immediate term and in the long run.

Alternatives include looking for "unblocking reforms," which entail governments looking to remove artificial barriers in their own societies to foster peaceful interaction and exchange with other countries (Coyne, 2013). For instance, the governments of Western countries might look to reduce or remove their own barriers to the free movement of goods and people (Boettke and Coyne, 2007). This does not require intervening in other societies but can still potentially offer significant benefits for human well-being. Ultimately, sustainable institutional change must be endogenous to the society within which it takes place (Boettke, Coyne, and Leeson, 2008).[7]

## 4 Counterterrorism: Three Dilemmas for a Liberal Society

Liberalism, from the Latin "liber" meaning "free," is the philosophy of individual freedom (Mises, 1996: v; McCloskey, 2019: 10; Boettke, 2021). Liberal societies are citizen driven; the liberty of individual citizens is a primary value. To the extent that government has a role, it is to protect citizens' liberty. Liberal democracies are characterized by freedom of association, freedom of speech, and economic freedom grounded in human dignity and toleration. They are also defined by political competition – that is, regularly scheduled elections, separation of political powers – and the rule of law, mechanisms intended to constrain government and limit abuses of power. Where institutions effectively check government power, the state is limited to protecting the person and property of the citizenry.

Terrorism and counterterrorism policy pose three unique challenges to liberal societies. The first relates to the vulnerability of liberal societies to terrorist threats. The second entails the possible erosion of liberal values associated with counterterrorism policies. The third relates to the threat of permanent expansions in domestic government power and the concomitant erosion of domestic liberty. We discuss each in turn.

### Dilemma 1: Vulnerability of Liberal Democracies

Starting with Eubank and Weinberg (1994), scholars have empirically examined the relationship between democracy and terrorism (see Eyerman, 1998; Abadie, 2006; Kurrild-Klitgaard, Justesen, and Klemmensen, 2006; Chenoweth, 2010; de la Calle and Sánchez-Cuenca, 2012; Piazza, 2013). A key finding of these studies is that terrorism is *more* prevalent in democratic societies. To many, these results seem counterintuitive. Democracies allow for political participation, elected representatives at a variety of political levels, and competitive elections that allow for turnover and turn taking. Intuitively, these factors should disincentivize terrorism because people can voice their grievances and turn to the halls of politics to seek change, as

---

[7] For a survey of Austrian contributions to the study of institutions, see Palagashvili, Piano, and Skarbek (2017).

opposed to resorting to violence. Some note that this reasoning overlooked a tension facing liberal democracies (Crenshaw, 1981; Schmid, 1992; Eubank and Weinberg, 1994; Enders and Sandler, 2012: 28–60). That is, the same defining features of liberal democracies that may reduce terrorist activity also make them uniquely vulnerable to the possibility of terrorism.

The freedoms (freedom of association, freedom of speech, and economic freedom) and the tolerance of alternative views and beliefs in liberal societies create space for terrorists – individuals and organizations – to act. As Enders and Sandler (2012: 28) note: "Ironically, a liberal democracy protects not only its citizens and residents but also the terrorists who engage in attacks on its soil. The political and civil freedoms that define a liberal democracy provide a favorable environment in which to wage terrorist campaigns."

Freedom of thought allows people to develop and hold a range of beliefs, including those that might motivate terrorism. Freedom of association allows people with shared beliefs to interact and form organizations and networks that can be leveraged for a multitude of purposes – both good and bad. Freedom of speech allows people to publicly express their views and beliefs to others, even if those views are believed to be radical or repugnant. Freedom of movement allows people to travel across geographic space, giving them greater access to other people, networks, and resources. These features of liberal democracies provide opportunities for terrorists to carry out the various aspects of their campaigns, from networking and recruitment to securing financing and resources to planning and carrying out actual acts of terrorism. Moreover, freedom of the press presents terrorists with the opportunity to receive publicity for their actions, which may enhance their ability to recruit and secure financing (Gadarian, 2010; Enders and Sandler, 2012: 43–48; Hoffman, 2017).

Recent empirical scholarship has attempted to disaggregate democracy to move beyond the binary democracy–autocracy split and offer more nuanced analyses (Chenoweth, 2013). When data are disaggregated, the existing literature finds that consolidated democracies do not generally suffer from persistent terrorism, with two exceptions. The first is cases where consolidated democracies engage in military intervention in other societies. In these cases, the intervening country experiences a greater frequency of terrorist attacks, which may be explained by retaliation against an intervening government. The second exception is poor democracies experiencing territory-related conflicts. In these cases, terrorism becomes one tool in the broader conflict. Chenoweth (2013: 375) presents the implications of these findings as follows: "If there is a common message emerging from recent research, it is that a country's best defense against terrorism is to enhance its legitimacy, not only through democratic practices but also through genuine liberal practices both at home and abroad." Of course, an appreciation for the central importance of liberal values and practices reveals a second dilemma emerging from government responses to terrorism.

## Dilemma 2: Erosion of Liberal Values

In responding to terrorist threats, democratic governments often adopt illiberal means in the pursuit of liberal ends. Coyne and Hall (2016a, 2018: 30–36) explore the "interventionist mindset" associated with a proactive foreign policy that is grounded in preparing for and intervening in other societies. This mindset requires the intervening government to be comfortable with the use of coercive force and violence against other human beings to achieve its goals. Success in foreign interventions "requires a willingness to use various techniques – monitoring, curfews, segregation, bribery, censorship, suppression, imprisonment, torture, violence, and so on – to control those who resist foreign governments or their goals" (Coyne and Hall, 2018: 30). To the extent that counterterrorism policy entails some form of foreign intervention, a similar illiberal mindset is required.

It may be the case that the adoption of illiberal methods is of minimal concern because they will be used as a last resort, and only in extreme cases where terrorist threats justify such measures. Even where governments attempt to limit the use of illiberal methods, however, there will be a tendency for counterterrorism activities to extend beyond their limited intentions. As one illustration, consider the use of torture as a counterterrorism technique. It is well documented that democratic governments not only use torture but were innovators in "clean torture" techniques – techniques that do not leave physical marks – in order to avoid detection through public monitoring (Rejali, 2007).[8] Examples of clean torture techniques include sleep deprivation, electro torture, water torture, and various forms of stress and duress.

The use of torture by liberal democratic governments is justified on the grounds that in some extreme cases – those that are often referred to as "ticking time bomb" scenarios – extreme measures are needed to protect citizens. Using game theory, Schiemann (2012, 2015) explores some of the likely outcomes of a government accepting and adopting the use of torture techniques as a form of counterterrorism. He concludes that the frequency and the intensity of torture will likely be greater than claimed, with questionable reliability of information obtained. The logic underlying his analysis is as follows.

---

[8] For more on the US government's use of torture, see McCoy (2007), Fair (2016), and Fallon (2017). For a first-hand account by a detainee at Guantanamo Bay detention camp, see Slahi (2015).

In thinking of torture and interrogation from a game theoretic approach, we may place players into one of two categories – "interrogators" and "detainees." Interrogators are assumed to be pragmatists, meaning they employ torture only in limited, extreme situations and only until the necessary information is obtained. In order to consider the best-case scenario, by assumption, this excludes the possibility of sadists who enjoy torture as a consumption good. Detainees can be one of three types: "knowledgeable and strong," "knowledgeable and weak," or "innocent." A knowledgeable and strong detainee knows relevant information but can withhold that information even when experiencing a relatively intense degree of torture. A knowledgeable and weak detainee possesses information and will succumb to torture by revealing information more quickly than a knowledgeable and strong detainee. Finally, an innocent detainee does not possess any relevant information and has nothing to reveal, no matter the intensity of the torture. Against this background, Schiemann considers claims about the frequency, intensity, and accuracy of information obtained under the use of torture.

First consider frequency. The interrogator suffers from an information asymmetry problem regarding the three potential types of detainees; they do not know to which category the detainee belongs. Innocent detainees do not possess relevant information and therefore cannot reveal anything. Knowledgeable and weak and knowledgeable and strong detainees possess information but will not reveal it to interrogators absent some positive amount of torture. The dilemma facing the interrogator is that they cannot always differentiate between the three detainee types. They may believe they have a knowledgeable detainee, but they may be mistaken, and the person might be innocent. In the face of information asymmetries, the interrogator will need to torture innocent people to ensure that they are not knowledgeable detainees who are pretending to be innocent.

Further incentivizing the frequency of torture is that the interrogator needs to establish a credible reputation for using torture; if they do not, the threat of torture will be empty and fail to incentivize the desired behavior. If the detainee has a sense that the interrogator will not carry through on the threat of torture, then knowledgeable detainees will be incentivized to act as if they are innocent. The incentive facing interrogators, therefore, is to use torture against innocent people both to establish a credible torture reputation and to separate the innocent from the knowledgeable.

Next consider the intensity of torture. When a detainee refuses to provide actionable information, it might be that they do not know anything relevant – that is, they are innocent – or it might be that the cost of torture is too low. If the cost of torture is too low, knowledge detainees, whether weak or strong, will not reveal information. If the interrogator believes that the detainee has information, their incentive is to increase the intensity of the torture to raise the cost of failing to reveal the information. The threshold of torture at which both weak and strong detainees reveal information is not uniform across detainees and cannot be known *ex ante*. The interrogator may believe that the failure to reveal information is the result of failure to meet this threshold such that the detainee is pretending to be innocent. The issue, of course, is that it is possible that they may genuinely be innocent. Once torture is introduced, not only will innocent people be tortured but the intensity of the torture they face will increase to separate them from knowledgeable detainees.

Finally, consider the issue of information reliability. Interrogators have to determine whether any information the detainee reveals is complete and accurate. They also need to establish a credible reputation for stopping torture when information is received. If detainees do not expect torture to stop after revealing accurate information, they have a weak incentive to reveal the information in the first place. The issues of frequency and intensity, therefore, run the risk of harming the reputation of the interrogator as one who ceases torture once accurate information is revealed. In the face of information asymmetries, the interrogator may choose to continue to torture to ensure that all relevant information has been revealed accurately. But this might disincentivize the revelation of actionable information.

Further compounding the issue of reliability is that there are often no immediate feedback mechanisms with which to "test" whether the information being provided is accurate. This is especially likely to be the case in ticking time bomb–type situations, which are the standard justification for the use of torture by liberal governments. Taken together, the main implication is that "although information from interrogational torture is unreliable, it is likely to be used frequently and harshly" once accepted as a counterterrorism policy (Schiemann, 2012: 3).

As the example of torture illustrates, counterterrorism policies are often illiberal. There is an inherent tension in employing illiberal policies in the name of liberal ends; embracing illiberal means erodes liberal values as the adopting government runs the risk of becoming the very thing it seeks to combat. A dilemma facing liberal societies, therefore, is whether, and how, counterterrorism policies threaten the very liberal values that they are intended to protect in the first place.

## Dilemma 3: Permanent Expansion of Government and Erosion of Domestic Liberty

In addition to threatening liberal values in a general sense, counterterrorism policies can pose a direct threat to domestic liberty. Hayek (1979: 124) recognized the broader concern about crisis situations threatening freedoms, noting that "'[e]mergencies' have always been the pretext on which the safeguards of

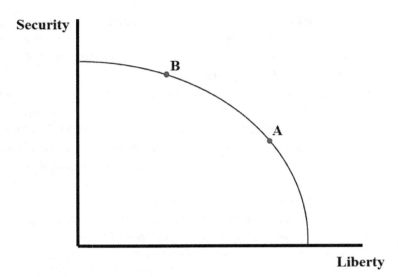

**Figure 2** Trade-Off Model

**Source:** Created by the authors.

individual liberty have been eroded – and once they are suspended it is not difficult for anyone who has assumed such emergency powers to see to it that the emergency will persist." To understand how government responses to emergencies can reduce domestic liberty, consider two models of the state in emergency situations.

### Trade-Off Model

The security–liberty trade-off model of state emergency powers (illustrated in Figure 2) has been applied to the US government's war on terror (see Posner and Vermeule, 2007; Coyne and Yatsyshina, 2021).[9] In this framework there is a straightforward trade-off between citizens' security and citizens' liberty, which are treated as aggregate categories. Government selects a mix of security activities that lies along a frontier representing alternative bundles of security and liberty. It is assumed that increases in state-provided security come at the expense of citizen liberty.

Government is also assumed to be a social welfare–maximizing apparatus. "The problem from the social point of view is to optimize: to choose the joint level of liberty and security that maximizes the aggregate welfare of the population" (Posner and Vermeule, 2007: 22). In the face of a legitimate threat,

---

[9] This section is based on Coyne and Yatsyshina (2021: 190–194).

the state adopts policies that increase the security of the citizenry while reducing its liberties. This is represented by a movement from Point A to Point B in Figure 2. The underlying logic is that as threats intensify, the benefit of more security, and less individual liberty, increases.

Another assumption of the trade-off model is the existence of well-functioning political mechanisms with which to select and adjust the appropriate mix of security and liberty. "As threats increase, the value of security increases; a rational and well-motivated government will then trade-off some losses in liberty for greater gains in increased security" (Posner and Vermeule, 2007: 27). As threats subside, the value of liberty, relative to security, increases, and there is movement down the frontier (back toward Point A).

Well-functioning political mechanisms, it is assumed, ensure equal treatment of citizens, preventing political opportunism in the form of discriminatory policy. "Officials do not systematically act as agents either for a majority or for a minority. Rather, the government impartially maximizes the welfare of all whose interests and preferences should count" (Posner and Vermeule, 2007: 30). These mechanisms also prevent systematic policy errors and abuses of state power; these are corrected by checks and balances such as Congressional oversight, judicial review, and citizen voting. The political process will also correct for suboptimal policies – represented by points inside the security–liberty frontier in Figure 2 – to enhance social welfare. The overall result of this framework is that government policymaking tends toward efficiency in terms of maximizing social welfare along the security–liberty dimension.

Two key categories of assumptions underlie the trade-off model. The first is that policymakers have the requisite knowledge for constructing a social welfare function that provides the optimal security–liberty mix. The second is that the political process will produce the appropriate political incentives to determine the optimal mix but also to produce policies that achieve that mix. Let us critically consider each of these assumptions in turn.

## Epistemic Constraints and the Social Welfare Function

A social welfare function aggregates and ranks the alternative states of the world, allowing the analyst to weigh a variety of ends and to determine the optimal allocation of scarce resources so as to maximize social welfare. Buchanan (1954, 1959, 1969) raises several challenges to the ability to construct and operationalize a social welfare function.[10] These challenges are grounded in the epistemic (knowledge) limitations facing policymakers,

---

[10] On the subjectivist roots of Buchanan's economics, see DiLorenzo, 1990.

a theme that is prevalent throughout the history of Austrian economics stemming back to the socialist calculation debate in the early twentieth century (for a summary see Coyne, 2020a: 20–24). The focus on knowledge constraints has been applied to a variety of government policy issues, including the ability of the government to determine the "optimal" levels of security and defense (see Coyne, 2015, 2020a; Coyne and Lucas, 2016; Coyne and Hall, 2019).

Individual utilities are not fixed and given, thus firmly limiting our ability to construct a social welfare function. "A necessary condition for deriving a social welfare function is that all possible states be ordered *outside* or *external* to the decision-making process itself. What is necessary, in effect, is that the one erecting such a function be able to translate the individual values (which are presumably revealed to him) into social building blocks" (Buchanan, 1954: 121–122, emphasis in original).

Individual valuations are subjective and in the mind of the individual actor and thus not available to the external observer for quantification (Buchanan, 1959, 1969). "Utility is measurable, ordinally or cardinally, only to the individual decision-maker. It is a subjectively quantifiable magnitude" (Buchanan, 1959: 126). This certainly applies to matters of security, which is an individualized and subjective concept consisting of many heterogeneous margins, as compared to a single aggregate category that applies to everyone equally. The implication of the subjectivism of utility is that the analyst "must remain fundamentally ignorant concerning the actual ranking of alternatives until and unless that ranking is revealed by the overt action of the individual in choosing" (Buchanan, 1959: 126).

Further complicating matters is that people's utility functions evolve through time as people experience the world. People have the ability to imagine the person they want to be and can take steps to become that person (Buchanan, 1979). The "prospects of becoming are sufficient to channel action, to divert resources away from the automatic routine that utility maximization, as normally presented, seems to embody ... We move through time, constructing ourselves ... We are not, and cannot be, the 'same person' in any utility maximization sense" (Buchanan, 1979: 100).

Human action in an open-ended system means that people can learn and act creatively to shape the person they are, the implication being that utility functions cannot be treated as fixed units of account that can be collected and summed up by an analyst. Instead, the external observer must judge and impose their ordering of preferences.

> Individual preferences, in so far as they enter the [social welfare] construction[,] must be those which appear to the observer rather than those revealed by the behavior of the individuals themselves. In other words, even if the value

judgments expressed in the function say that individual preferences are to count, these preferences must be those presumed by the observer rather than those revealed in behavior. (Buchanan, 1959: 126)

Taken together, the implications are as follows. Due to the inability to construct a genuine social welfare function, there is no optimal aggregate security–liberty mix that can be determined by experts. Instead, policymakers must impose their valuations and judgments on members of society. This shifts the focus to the political processes through which security policy is designed and implemented.

## Political Process

The political process determines security policy in the context of the security–liberty trade-off model. This process is characterized by the interaction of several categories of actors – individual voters, special interest groups, elected officials, and members of Congress, the judiciary, and government bureaus. The individuals constituting these categories are embedded in institutions that shape the incentives they face. Existing scholarship notes that the operations of political institutions are characterized by a variety of frictions that influence the design and implementation of policy (see Buchanan, 1954; Mueller, 2003; Rowley and Schneider, 2004; Reksulak, Razzolini, and Shughart, 2014; Wagner and Yazigi, 2014).

Appreciating political frictions matters for two reasons. First, they call into question and challenge the assumption that policies that maximize social welfare will be selected. Second, once adopted, inefficient policies tend to be sticky and costly to reverse. In the context of the security–liberty trade-off, this means that once a government expands its power (and reduces individual liberty as a result) in the name of security, it will be expensive to undo it. Endogenous processes will incentivize maintaining and expanding the status quo, leading to yet more state power and less liberty, compared to the prior situation.

Following Coyne and Hall (2021: 25–33), in what follows we consider the key political stakeholders involved in designing and implementing security policy. Although we consider each general category in the context of the United States, these insights are applicable across political systems and governments.

### Individual Voters

In a democratic system, individual voting is typically seen as a central check on the behaviors of elected representatives. The underlying logic is that voters can reward or punish elected officials at the voting booth. There are four issues that weaken the effectiveness of voting in disciplining elected representatives.

The first is the information deficiency of voters. The incentive for voters to acquire and process information to hold elected officials accountable is weak due to the low likelihood that a vote will influence the outcome of an election (see Downs, 1957; Bohanon and Van Cott, 2002; Heckelman, 2003; Gelman, Silver, and Edlin, 2012; Somin, 2013; Brennan, 2016).

The second, related issue is that even if voters want to be informed, they are limited in the realm of foreign policy because of extensive secrecy (see Coyne, Goodman, and Hall, 2019; Coyne and Hall, 2021: 33–37). The national security activities of the state tend to be shrouded in confidentiality, making it difficult, if not impossible for even the most interested citizens to understand what is happening, let alone make the kind of clear connections to specific activities and outcomes that are crucial for accountability.

A third factor limiting the effectiveness of voting as a check on government is "bundling." Each voter casts a single vote for a candidate who represents a collection, or bundle, of nuanced and complex policies. There is no way for a voter to unbundle these policies to express satisfaction or dissatisfaction on certain issues. For example, a single vote cannot simultaneously communicate satisfaction with education policy and dissatisfaction with foreign policy.

The fourth factor is the timing between elections for federal offices – president, vice president, and US Congress. Boudreaux (1996: 117) notes that over each six-year period, a US voter has a maximum of nine votes over four elections. Even if voters can identify clear connections between specific actors and outcomes, the issue of timing makes it difficult for them to provide timely feedback to elected officials. Further, by the time an election occurs, it may very well be impossible to undo the undesirable outcomes (Higgs, 2012: 34–46). Policies, and especially those related to national security, have extensive effects that change the fabric of society. While some policies can be altered by newly elected officials, many changes resulting from past decisions cannot simply be undone. This means that if voters are unhappy with an official, they can vote against them, but this does not reverse what has already occurred and the often long-lasting effects of those decisions.

Consider the case of President George W. Bush. Leading up to the 2000 presidential election, there was no way for voters to anticipate the September 11, 2001 attacks or to evaluate the Bush administration's potential response. Further, by the time of the 2004 election there was no way that the extensive "war on terror" and its effect on nearly all facets of life could be entirely undone, even if a large majority of voters desired this outcome. As already discussed, various institutional and ideological changes tend to make past political policies and choices difficult to reverse (Higgs, 1987, 2008; Coyne and Hall, 2018). This reality, in combination with the prior factors, weakens the effectiveness of the voting booth as a means of voters expressing their preferences and holding politicians accountable. The result is that policymakers will not select the security–liberty mix that maximizes social welfare because they lack both knowledge of voter preferences and incentive to implement policies accordingly.

### Special Interest Groups

A special interest group is a collection of voters who join together for a common goal. While individual voters typically face the incentive to remain uniformed about the specifics of security policy, special interest groups have a stronger incentive to be informed about policy and to attempt to influence it. By joining together in an interest group, voters can leverage their increased political power by exchanging their support for favorable policies (Olson, 1965). Interest groups operate by concentrating politically generated benefits on their members while spreading costs among a large number of taxpaying citizens.

Perhaps the most well-known example of an interest group in the realm of national security is the "military-industrial-congressional complex" (MICC), which refers to the iron triangle between the government's military apparatus, Congress, and private industry and special interests (e.g., unions).[11] These connections allow for members of the iron triangle to influence and shape security policy. Similar logic underpins John Mueller's (2006) discussion of the "terrorism industry," which includes members of the government, private industry, and the media, which has an interest in perpetuating and extending the US government's "war on terror."

### Elected Officials

To remain in power, politicians must win the votes necessary for election or reelection. They will therefore seek to adopt policies to satisfy some combination of the median voter (the voter located in the middle of the ideological distribution) and special interest groups. Elected officials will focus on the key segments of their constitutions in order to get elected. This is important because elected officials will often advocate for policies that benefit their constituents even when they are at odds with some notion of the "national interest" and "national security."

To illustrate this point, consider the reflections of Robert Gates, a former secretary of defense who served under both President George W. Bush and President Barack Obama. Recounting his experience with members of Congress, he recalled:

---

[11] On the MICC and its effects, see Melman (1970, 1974), Higgs (2006), Duncan and Coyne (2013a, 2013b, 2015), and McCartney and McCartney (2015).

> I was more or less continuously outraged by the parochial self-interest of all but a very few members of Congress. Any defense facility or contract in their district or state, no matter how superfluous or wasteful, was sacrosanct. I was constantly amazed and infuriated at the hypocrisy of those who most stridently attacked the Defense Department as inefficient and wasteful but fought tooth and nail to prevent any reduction in defense activities in their home state or district. (Gates, 2014: n.p.)

As this suggests, each elected official is incentivized to pursue their own narrow interests, which often do not align with the interests of people residing outside their constituency. This is problematic because elected officials are supposed to work together for the common good of the common defense.

## Congressional Oversight

In principle, Congressional representatives can advance the interests of their constituent voters by checking the behaviors of the executive and government agencies. There are four factors limiting the effectiveness of members of Congress in this role (Coyne, 2018; Coyne and Hall, 2018: 58; Coyne, Goodman, and Hall, 2019). First, members of Congress are often reliant for information on the very members of the national security state they are tasked with overseeing. This allows those being monitored to control the flow and content of the information shared.

Second, some of the main decision-makers of the security state are not subject to Congressional oversight. One example of this is the position of national security advisor. As a senior aide to the US president, the person in this position has significant influence over security policy. The position is not subject to Congressional confirmation or oversight.

Third, many members of Congress are limited in understanding the nuanced operations of the national security state. Part of this is due to the complexity and breadth of the national security state itself. Part is due to the wide array of demands on Congressional members across a range of policy issues. Members of Congress often have an incentive to see the national security state persist and expand, especially when it directly benefits their constituents.

## Judicial Review

Judicial review, whereby courts evaluate whether an action by the government is legal, is also an imperfect mechanism for ensuring the optimal security–liberty policy mix (see Coyne, 2018; Coyne and Hall, 2018: 59–60). One issue is that during times of emergency the courts tend to become aligned with and deferential to the other branches of government (see Fraenkel, 1946; Dorsen, 1989; Rehnquist, 1998). During World War II, for instance, the Supreme Court "gave judicial sanction to whatever powers and actions the President and Congress found necessary to the prosecution of the war" (Rossiter, 2009 [1948]: 265). In general, Corwin (1947: 177) argues that "the Court necessarily loses some part of its normal freedom of decision and becomes assimilated, like the rest of society, to the mechanism of national defense." This is especially relevant in situations such as the US government's "war on terror," which is open-ended and with no clear notion of what victory would look like.

Glennon (2015) notes that in many instances there may be a bias in the judiciary toward the security state. The reason is that "[j]udicial nominees often come from the ranks of prosecutors, law enforcement, and national security officials, and they have often participated in the same sorts of activities the lawfulness of which they will later be asked to adjudicate" (Glennon, 2015: 40). The federal judiciary is composed of former advocates of government, rather than civil liberty or criminal defense attorneys, by a factor of seven to one (Neily, 2021). To the extent that such biases exist, preference will be given to the maintenance and expansion of the security state over the liberty of private people.

### Government Bureaus

Bureaucrats are nonelected political actors. Security policy is implemented and influenced through an extensive bureaucratic apparatus (see Priest and Arkin, 2011). Bureaus are nonprofit government agencies; in the absence of a profit motive, there is an incentive to focus on other metrics of success. This includes the size of the discretionary budget – the portion of the budget beyond what is necessary to satisfy the demand of legislators (Niskanen, 1971, 1975, 2001). A larger budget allows bureaus to exert influence, hire more employees, and increase their activities (see Tullock, 1965; Wagner, 2007). Bureaus face a strong incentive to spend, even if that spending is wasteful, in order to demonstrate to legislators and the public that they are "doing something" and to enable them to lobby for larger budgets in the future. Bennett (2017), for instance, catalogs numerous examples of post-9/11 homeland security spending that has little to do with advancing even the most elastic concept of national security.

Congressional oversight of bureaus is limited for the reasons discussed earlier (Coyne and Hall, 2021: 31–32). There are (often severe) information asymmetries between members of Congress and the bureaus that control the flow of information. To provide one example, the Pentagon concealed a study revealing that $125 billion could potentially be saved by reducing waste for fear that Congress would cut its budget (see Whitlock and Woodward, 2016).

Moreover, members of Congress often have an incentive to support the expansion of national security bureaus. "The Armed Services Committee has a tradition of uniting its members on both sides of the aisle, since many have a military background or home-state interests in defense" (Steinhauer, 2015: n.p.). This matters because once the government expands the scale and scope of its security policies, there are dynamics that will tend to make changes persist and grow further.

### Summing Up: Implications of Political Pathologies

The various pathologies of the political process can lead to the design and implementation of security policies that are highly dysfunctional and fail in their stated goal of protecting the person and property of citizens. Former secretary of defense Robert Gates captured these pathologies when he recounted the following based on his experience trying to navigate the policy process related to the US wars in Afghanistan and Iraq as part of the larger war on terror:

> I did not just have to wage war in Afghanistan and Iraq and against al-Qaeda; I also had to battle the bureaucratic inertia of the Pentagon, surmount internal conflicts within both administrations, avoid the partisan abyss in Congress, evade the single-minded parochial self-interest of so many members of Congress and resist the magnetic pull exercised by the White House, especially in the Obama administration, to bring everything under its control and micromanagement. (Gates, 2014: n.p.)

Political pathologies are especially costly where the price of supposed increased security is reductions in liberty. The cost is even greater because once government power has been expanded, and liberty reduced, there are endogenous incentives that make the change lasting and resistant to reversion. A full analysis of counterterrorism policy, therefore, needs to take this into account. The ratchet effect model of government responses to crises, to which we now turn, offers an alternative to the trade-off model and provides a clear avenue for incorporating these realities.

### Ratchet Effect Model: An Alternative

The security–liberty trade-off model suggests that once a threat subsides, the government will divest its security powers and increase citizen liberty (movement from Point B toward Point A in Figure 2). However, the various frictions that exist in the political process mean that the movement between various security–liberty mixes is anything but smooth and efficient. Once the state grasps more power in the name of security, these frictions may prevent the full divesture of those powers in future periods. State responses to national emergencies have real effects on the fabric of domestic life that cannot simply be undone at will (see Higgs, 1987, 2004, 2007, 2012; Coyne and Hall, 2018). This reality is captured in the ratchet effect model of state responses to emergencies, as developed by Higgs (1987) and illustrated in Figure 3.

The vertical axis represents the size of the government inclusive of both scale *and* scope. Scale refers to the size of the government as captured by indicators such as expenditure or number of people employed. Scope captures the range and extent of the activities undertaken by the state. Scale and scope might be correlated, but this is not necessarily the case. For instance, advances in technology may enable states to engage in more extensive surveillance activities than previously with the same, or an even smaller, budget. The horizontal axis represents the time element of some emergency or crisis situation. The logic behind each stage of the model is as follows (see Higgs, 1987: 60–62):

Stage 1 (Points A to B) is precrisis normalcy; this is the path of government growth that would occur absent the emergency situation. Stage 2 (Points B to C) is government expansion as the state responds to the crisis situation. Stage 3 (Points C to D) represents the maturity of the emergency situation, while Stage 4 (Points D to E) captures the retrenchment of the government as the crisis subsides. Crucially, the postcrisis size of the government and the subsequent path of growth (Points E to F) are larger compared to the no-emergency counterfactual (Points B to F*). This gap represents the increase, or permanent ratchet upward, in the size of the government due to the crisis response.

The permanent expansion in the size of the government is due to several factors. The first is the expansion of existing government bureaus and the creation of new agencies. An example is illustrative. The Department of Homeland Security (DHS) was founded in the wake of the September 11, 2001 attacks to coordinate the federal government's homeland security activities. It is now one of the largest Cabinet departments (after the DOD and Veterans Affairs) and will likely remain in existence even if the government's "war on terror" subsides. In general, the government's activities create new vested interests, and those interests have an incentive to continue their operations even after the initial emergency evolves or ends.

The ideologies of the members of society – citizens, elected officials, the judiciary, and nonelected bureaucrats – also play a key role in the permanent expansion in the size of the government (Higgs, 1987, 2008). Ideology refers to "a somewhat coherent, rather comprehensive belief system about social relations" (Higgs, 1987: 37). This includes the relationship between the citizen and the state. Ideology changes as the emergency-related activities of the government become normalized in everyday life.

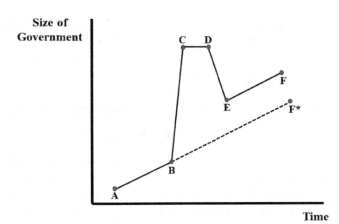

**Figure 3** Ratchet effect model

**Source:** Created by the authors.

One example of this is the new airport security measures implemented in the United States following the September 11 attacks. For most travelers, these new rules, which would have seemed excessive, if not obnoxious, prior to the attacks, have become a routine part of traveling. Those born either not long before the attacks or after the attacks know of nothing different since they did not experience precrisis life. For them, post-9/11 government activities, which are expansive compared to the pre-9/11 period, are normal life.

In other instances, the crisis response creates new opportunities for some people, both inside and outside of government, to benefit. This makes them more accepting of the larger size of the government and the new civilian–state relationship. Those in the "terrorism industry," for instance, who benefit from the government's "war on terror" are more likely to be ideologically supportive of the expanded size of the government because they personally profit and view themselves as contributing to "the nation's" security.

Together, these ideological changes support the persistence of the increase in the overall size of the government postcrisis. Some aspects of the emergency response will recede. However, it is possible that the overall size of the government will not return to its precrisis growth path. This suggests that the government's response to a crisis cannot simply be reversed at the flip of a switch. Ideologies, interests, and the citizen–civilian relationship have all changed in ways that limit the ability to return to "how things were" prior to the emergency. To return to the security–liberty trade-off framework, the Point A situation (Figure 2) may likely not be an option to return to after the move is made to Point B (more security, less liberty) because of institutional and ideological changes.

With this in mind, we turn to the September 11, 2001 terrorist attacks in the United States and the subsequent "war on terror." We consider whether the government response has succeeded in its stated goals and discuss some of the long-lasting effects on American society.

## 5 The War on Terror: A Twenty-Year Assessment

### The 9/11 Terror Attacks

On the morning of September 11, 2001, nineteen militants associated with al-Qaeda carried out the deadliest terror attack in US history.[12] Groups of attackers boarded four domestic US aircraft at three airports on the eastern coast of the United States. Soon after takeoff, the hijackers took control of the planes. At 8:46 a.m., American Airlines flight 11 was flown into the north tower of the World Trade Center in New York City. Seventeen minutes later, United Airlines flight 175 was piloted into the south tower of the World Trade Center. A third aircraft, American Airlines flight 77, left Dulles International Airport in Virginia only to crash into the Pentagon just outside of Washington, DC, at 9:37 a.m. The impact collapsed the west side of the building. The fourth plane, United Airlines flight 93, crashed in a field in Pennsylvania. Passengers, told of the other attacks via cell phone, attempted to thwart the hijacking. At 9:59 a.m., the south tower of the World Trade Center collapsed, followed by the north tower twenty-nine minutes later. Other buildings suffered serious damage or collapsed due to compromised structural integrity. The subsequent fires at the site of the World Trade Center burned for more than three months (for a more comprehensive account of the attacks, see Bergen, n.d.).

The attacks resulted in substantial civilian losses, making them the deadliest attacks on domestic soil in US history. Some 2,750 people died in New York City, including more than 400 first responders (primarily police and firefighters) who had gone to the scene as part of rescue efforts. Outside of Washington, DC, 184 were killed as a result of the attack on the Pentagon. The forty people aboard United Flight 93 also died (Bergen, n.d.) In addition to these immediate fatalities, thousands more were injured. According to the Global Terrorism Database, the 4 attacks resulted in nearly 11,000 injuries (Global Terrorism Database, 2021).

The health effects of the attacks extended well beyond the immediate days and months following. One study of more than 8,000 adult survivors of the attacks on the World Trade Center found that more than half (56.6 percent) reported either "new or worsening respiratory symptoms … 23.9% had

---

[12] This section takes Coyne (2021) as its basis.

heartburn/reflux, and 21.0% had severe headaches" (Hampton, 2006: n.p.). A study of more than 36,000 survivors likewise found higher rates of respiratory problems like asthma, coughing, wheezing, and reflux. Some 14.2 percent of the individuals studied met the study criteria for post-traumatic stress disorder (PTSD) and 15.3 percent exhibited signs of depression (see Jordan et al., 2019).

The 9/11 terror attacks represent a critical event in US history as a whole. Their importance with respect to contemporary counterterrorism policy – both domestic and international – cannot be understated. The changes implemented by the US government in the immediate aftermath of the attacks and in the years following permanently altered US counterterrorism efforts and the US government as a whole.

### Start of the War on Terror

Five days after the attacks, President George W. Bush spoke from the South Lawn of the White House. "My administration has a job to do, and we're going to do it. We will rid the world of evil-doers" (Bush, 2001a: n.p.). Several days later, the president addressed members of Congress. He made his policy intentions clear and officially launched the "war on terror," stating: "Whether we bring our enemies to justice, or bring justice to our enemies, justice will be done" (Bush, 2001b: n.p.). Making extensive references to al-Qaeda and Afghanistan, he said: "These demands are not open to negotiation or discussion . . .. They [the Taliban] will hand over the terrorists, or they will share in their fate" (Bush, 2001b: n.p.).

The war on terror refers not to any single military conflict or program but to a mix of both domestic and international policies and operations related to terrorism. The US Congress never officially declared war on terrorism. It did, however, issue the Authorization for Use of Military Force (AUMF) on September 18, 2001. Citing the 9/11 attacks, the AUMF authorized the president to use "all necessary and appropriate force against those nations, organizations, or persons he determines planned, authorized, committed, or aided the terrorist attacks that occurred on September 11, 2001 . . . in order to prevent any future acts of international terrorism against the United States" (Public Law 107–40, 2001). Congress passed a separate AUMF in 2002, granting the president authority to "use the Armed Forces of the United States as he determines necessary" to defend the country against the "threat posed by Iraq" (Public Law 107–243, 2001).

Unsurprisingly, these two Congressional acts paved the way for two formal international conflicts. The United States invaded Afghanistan in October 2001 under Operation Enduring Freedom. In March 2003, the United States began

Operation Iraqi Freedom, in which the United States invaded Iraq and toppled the regime of Saddam Hussein. It would be incorrect, however, to assume that these two well-known conflicts were the only external operations related to the war on terror. As part of its global counterterrorism campaign, the US government conducted operations in parts of Africa, Yemen, and the Philippines. The United States returned its attentions to Iraq (along with Syria) in 2014 amid concerns regarding IS. Following the overthrow and death of Muammar Gaddafi in Libya four years prior, the United States launched Operation Unified Protector in 2014. More recently, between 2018 and 2020, the United States engaged in various global counterterrorism efforts (e.g., counterterrorism training, military exercises, combat operations, drone and air strikes) in eighty-five separate countries – mostly in Africa and the Middle East (see Savell, 2021). For perspective, this means that the United States intervened in 44 percent *of all nations on the planet* in a span of three years as part of the war on terror.

The war on terror is not relegated to foreign policy. In fact, some of the most significant components of US counterterrorism policy are focused domestically. A few days after the 9/11 attacks, President Bush announced the formation of a new department – the Office of Homeland Security (OHS). Less than a month after the attacks, on October 8, 2001, the office officially opened. The OHS, created to "develop and coordinate the implementation of a comprehensive national strategy to secure the United States from terrorist threats or attacks," was replaced by the DHS in November 2002 (Executive Order 13228, 2001). The DHS absorbed twenty-two distinct agencies with missions related to disaster response, border control, law enforcement, maritime security, and infrastructure. The Senate Appropriations Committee provided $69.85 billion for the department for financial year 2021 (United States Senate Committee on Appropriations, 2020: 1). The agency's budget was a "mere" $19.5 billion in 2002 (United States Department of Homeland Security, 2003: 30). At the time of its establishment, the DHS employed some 180,000 (United States Department of Homeland Security, 2004: 5); by 2021, it hosted some 240,000 employees (United States Department of Homeland Security, 2021). Discussing all the activities of the DHS would be remarkably difficult and beyond the scope of this Element. Given the number of agencies under the department's purview and the organization's total budget, it is not difficult to imagine the sheer magnitude of the agency's activities. Here, we discuss several components of DHS programs and agencies in more detail.

In addition to the formation of the OHS and, subsequently, the DHS, the US government's internal counterterrorism efforts expanded widely in other areas as well. In October 2001, Congress passed the Uniting and Strengthening America by Providing Appropriate Tools Required to Intercept and Obstruct

Terrorism Act, known more commonly as the USA PATRIOT Act (even more simply, the PATRIOT Act) (H.R. 3162, 2001). Intended to correct a variety of "intelligence failures" that contributed to the 9/11 attacks, the PATRIOT Act allowed for government agencies like the Federal Bureau of Investigation (FBI) and the National Security Agency (NSA) to gather and share data in ways they previously had not. For example, following the passage of the PATRIOT Act, government agents were able to access things like internet search histories and library records with minimal or no oversight. An individual's home could be searched without notification. Probable cause was no longer required for things like wiretapping a phone line.

The PATRIOT Act, the DHS, and military interventions abroad illustrate a number of the concepts outlined in Section 4. In discussing the PATRIOT Act, for example, Enders and Sandler (2012: 319) make explicit reference to the supposed trade-off between liberty and safety: "The USA PATRIOT Act traded off personal freedoms for collective security – a trade-off that some in the country were willing to make in light of the threat of future terrorism." Each of the three counterterrorism policy categories – income-based, price-based, and opportunity cost–based – is well represented throughout the PATRIOT Act and the DHS. Discussing changes in financial regulations following the 9/11 attacks, Gjoza (2019: 173) highlights how components of the PATRIOT Act sought to limit the financial means of terror groups: "[T]he counterterrorism component of financial policing became increasingly important [after 9/11]. Under section 311 of the [PATRIOT Act] . . . the U.S. Treasury [can] designate any financial institution in the world a 'money laundering concern' and prevent it from doing business with US banks or accessing the dollar system." The creation of the Transportation Security Administration (TSA) is a prime example of a price-based counterterrorism policy. The creation of the agency itself (one of the many under the umbrella of the DHS) as well as the implementation of any number of specific policies (e.g., scanning passengers' shoes, setting liquid allowances, using advanced imaging technology (AIT), etc.) illustrate attempts to "harden" passenger aircraft as targets against a potential attack. Section 3 offered an example of an opportunity cost–based counterterrorism approach when discussing the US war in Afghanistan. The DHS, however, sought to extend these policies beyond that single conflict. In 2016, the DHS announced that it would be awarding up to $10 million in grants to combat domestic extremism. In announcing the grants, former secretary of homeland security Jeh Johnson highlighted how the funds would be used for "developing resilience" and "challenging the narrative" of various terrorist groups like IS and neo-Nazis (Johnson, 2016).

In addition to offering clear examples of the different types of counterterrorism policies, the internal and external facets of the war on terror also illustrate the ratchet effect discussed by Higgs (1987). Utilizing the crises presented by the 9/11 attacks, the US government undertook a massive expansion in both scale and scope. Roos (2020: n.p.) captures this idea succinctly: "Consumed by fear, grief and outrage, America turned to its leaders for action. Congress and the White House answered with an unprecedented expansion of military, law enforcement and intelligence powers aimed at rooting out and stopping terrorists, at home and abroad."

### Measuring Success in the War on Terror

When President Bush declared war on terrorism in 2001, he set a clear – and bold – standard for success. "Our war on terror begins with al Qaeda, but it does not end there," he said. "It will not end *until every terrorist group of global reach has been found, stopped, and defeated*" (Bush, 2001b, emphasis added). So has the war on terror been successful? By the standard that President Bush set forth, the answer is plainly no. Consider that between 2018 and 2019 (the most recent data available) the Global Terrorism Database logged some 917 instances of terrorism globally (Global Terrorism Database 2021). Given that terrorism has existed in some form for thousands of years, eradication of terrorism is not a plausible aim (see Chaliand and Blin, 2016; Law, 2015).

Setting aside Bush's overly ambitious goal for the war on terror, what can be said about the relative success or failure of US counterterrorism policy in the post-9/11 period? Perhaps surprisingly, providing an accurate assessment of the war's success or failure is exceptionally difficult. This is due, in part, to a lack of clear criteria for success. Consider one 2007 report from the US Government Accountability Office (GAO) that read: "Among the various U.S. government agencies involved in anti-terrorism efforts, there is currently no common set of criteria for measuring success" (Perl, 2007: 2). The 9/11 Commission Report, published in 2004, does contain a section titled "Measuring Success." The section, however, "neither highlighted any measure currently in use by the government nor did it propose any" (quoted in Goepner, 2016: 109).

Lacking a consistent system of measurement with which to adjudicate between successes and failures in the war on terror is an obvious problem as there is no way to systematically observe changes over time. Even if such metrics were established, however, additional measurement problems would remain. The same GAO report, for example, noted several other measurement issues when it comes to counterterrorism policy. For instance, suppose the United States undertook operations leading to the death of senior-level terrorists. While the elimination of such targets could be viewed as a success, it is not clear what the overall outcome of such an action would likely be. "[I]f one terminates 2/3 of the senior leadership of a particular terrorist organization," the report suggests, "the ranks of the organization may grow and decentralize ... *evolving into a more resilient adversary*" (Perl, 2007: 5, emphasis added). The report also notes inherent problems with creating success metrics after a given policy has been implemented. "[S]uccess [should not be] defined retrospectively, with goals reformulated after the fact to correspond with the known outcomes" (Perl, 2007: 9).

This tendency of officials to redefine success is another barrier to critically assessing the outcomes of the war on terror. Writing on the war in Afghanistan, for example, former member of the US secretary of state's planning staff Daniel Twining noted: "[T]he Obama administration is attempting to shift the goalposts in Afghanistan away from building a functioning democracy and toward the limited objective of denying terrorists sanctuary on Afghan soil .... U.S. objectives have been defined away from nation-building, promoting good governance, and fostering long-term development" (Twining, 2009: n.p.). The problem is clear. Without an effective way to measure success or failure, different administrations, agencies, or individuals may change what constitutes a "victory" or a "defeat" in the war on terror.

Despite these challenges, some studies have attempted to measure success. The overall picture is not promising, though. Pointing to the massive expansion in counterterrorism policies following 9/11, Lum, Kennedy, and Sherley (2006: 489) conducted a systematic analysis of the research evaluating counterterrorism strategies and found "almost a complete absence of evaluation research on counter-terrorism interventions." Moreover, "from those evaluations that we could find, it appears that some interventions either did not achieve the outcomes sought or sometimes increased the likelihood of terrorism occurring" (Lum, Kennedy, and Sherley, 2006: 489). Colonel Eric Goepner (US Air Force, retired) also sought to answer the question of relative success in the war on terror. Using the stated objectives of Presidents Bush and Obama and the objectives outlined in various strategic documents, he contends that "objectives have remained consistent over time .... [T]hey include, protecting Americans, preventing terror attacks, defeating specific terror groups, and diminishing conditions that fuel terrorism" (Goepner, 2016: 108). He notes that prior attempts at measuring success have been "disjointed," and argues that "assessments of the war [on terror] will often devolve into flattery without substance" (Goepner, 2016: 110). In assessing the United States' counterterrorism policy post-9/11, Goepner (2016: 111) finds:

The data strongly suggest US efforts have had a significant and negative impact on terrorism over the last fifteen years. Increased US efforts are correlated with *a worsening of the overall terror situation* .... [F]or every additional billion dollars spent and 1,000 American troops sent to fight the war on terror, the number of terror attacks worldwide increased by 19 .... *[U]p to 80 percent of the variation in the number of worldwide terror attacks since 9/11 can be explained by just those two variables* – US money spent and military members sent to fight the war on terror. (emphasis added)

As these two studies note, the analyses of counterterrorism policy that can be made indicate that US efforts following 9/11 may have not only failed to achieve their stated goals but made the problem *worse*. This runs directly counter to the standard narrative of how governments plan, conduct, and review counterterrorism policy. Under the security–liberty trade-off model outlined in Section 4, a government, acting to maximize social welfare, would undertake policies that provide optimal amounts of security and liberty – with the assumption that "more safety" (in the form of enhanced counterterrorism efforts) would be met with less liberty. This would indicate, however, that the US government has likely failed to provide enhanced security. The marked expansion of a government into domestic life is undoubtedly a reduction in liberty. It follows, therefore, that, as opposed to trading off some amount of liberty for safety, the US government has acted so as to engender a reduction in both areas.

How do we explain this reduction? The answer lies in the epistemic constraints facing policymakers and the incentives generated by the political process. Next, we discuss in more detail a number of implications of US counterterrorism policy, analyzing the impacts of both internal and external counterterrorism policies.

## Implications of the War on Terror: Effects Abroad

As noted already, the United States has undertaken numerous interventions abroad as part of its post-9/11 counterterrorism policy, with operations in at least eighty-five separate nations (see Savell, 2021). We begin our discussion of the failures of US counterterrorism policy and the consequences these policies generate with a discussion of two of these foreign interventions.

First, consider the case of Libya, a country that from 1979 to 2006 occupied a place on the US list of "states sponsoring terrorism." For a country to be designated a state sponsor of terrorism, the US secretary of state must determine that it has "repeatedly provided support for acts of international terrorism" (United States Department of State, 2021). In March 2011, the United States and other nations carried out airstrikes against supporters of Libyan head of state Muammar Gaddafi and critical infrastructure targets amid the country's civil war. Rebel forces captured the capital city of Tripoli in August and Gaddafi was killed by rebel forces two months later. Though initially hailed as a success, US operations in Libya are a prime illustration of the knowledge problem of top-down planning and how these failures can have far-reaching effects.

Far from stabilizing the country, Gaddafi's death resulted in a power vacuum with rivaling factions vying for control. In addition to creating a crisis in Libya itself, US operations also fostered a positive disaster in the neighboring countries as well. Tuareg forces had staged a rebellion in Mali in 2007. Their efforts had been unsuccessful and many of the rebels had found sanctuary in Libya, where they received training and employment as part of Gaddafi's armed forces. After the collapse of the Gaddafi regime, these rebels returned to Mali and resumed their insurrection – only this time they brought military training and weaponry with them. Removing Gaddafi from power presented other neighboring countries – namely, Niger and Algeria – with similar concerns about Tuareg groups within their own geographic borders (see Larémont, 2013).

In addition to these consequences, US engagement in Libya had other direct negative consequences for US counterterrorism policy. Security and strategic studies scholar Andrea Beccaro, (2020: 8) notes that the "political havoc and instability" following the fall of the Gaddafi regime "paved the way for ISIS in 2014." But IS was not the only terror group to seek refuge in war-torn Libya: "ISIS was just one of several jihadist groups .... ISIS sent into Libya its foreign fighters with war experience gained in Iraq and Syria" (Beccaro, 2020: 8). Discussing the importance of post-Gaddafi Libya for terror groups, Sherine El Taraboulsi-McCarthy and coauthors state: "[A]fter the fall of the Gaddafi regime[, Libya's geographic] position became particularly strategic [for terror groups]. For several years [ISIS] has used the country as a base for its fight elsewhere in the region and as a training ground for new fighters" (El Taraboulsi-McCarthy et al., 2019: 6). Offering remarks to the US House Subcommittee on Africa, Global Health, and Human Rights, Christopher H. Smith noted that, following the fall of the Gaddafi regime, some Tuareg groups developed explicit ties to Islamic extremist groups, which posed a serious risk to the region as a whole: "The Tuaregs have been in conflict with the Central Government in Bamako, Mali for many years, but following [their mercenary service under Gaddafi] and increasing ties to al-Qaeda ... they now pose a danger, not only to Mali, but also to Algeria, Niger, Mauritania, Burkina Faso, and perhaps even Nigeria" (quoted in US House Subcommittee on Africa, Global Health, and Human Rights, 2012). In his testimony, he discussed how the region's instability similarly fostered organized terrorism: "Tuareg groups that were leading a rebellion in [northern

Mali] used the political crisis to effectively partition the country in two. The terrorism threat with which Mali had been struggling prior to the outbreak of the rebellion has grown as al-Qaeda in the Islamic Maghreb (AQIM), and other extremist groups have taken advantage of the power vacuum" (quoted in US House Subcommittee on Africa, Global Health, and Human Rights, 2012).

Reflecting on his time in office, former president Barack Obama stated that the worst mistake of his presidency was "failing to plan for the day after . . . intervening in Libya" (quoted in Karuri, 2016: n.p.). As this quote and the above details illustrate, planners were sorely limited in their knowledge of how their interventions would impact not only Libya but the region. Far from ushering in an era of stability and reducing the threat of terrorism, US efforts achieved the exact opposite outcome. Libya continues to struggle. Once an appealing destination for migrant workers and refugees, the country is now of interest to migrants only insofar as its vast coastline is used as a launching point for attempts to enter Europe, which has contributed to a number of migrant deaths and an overwhelming humanitarian crisis (see Stephen, 2016). Those fleeing the country are but some of those displaced since the fall of Gaddafi. Some 400,000 Libyans have been internally dislocated since 2014 (El Taraboulsi-McCarthy et al., 2019: 11).

Libya is not the only example of how US policies abroad in the war on terror served to undermine US strategic goals. Perhaps nowhere are the epistemological failures of US counterterrorism policy more on display than in the case of Afghanistan. Acting on the AUMF issued in September of that year, US forces (along with British support) invaded Afghanistan in October 2001. Writing on US policy and post-Taliban governance in the country, the Congressional Research Service summarizes the decision to invade Afghanistan succinctly: "After the September 11 attacks, the Bush Administration decided to militarily overthrow the Taliban when it refused . . . to extradite [Osama] Bin Laden. President Bush . . . asserted that a friendly regime in Kabul was needed to enable U.S. forces to search for Al Qaeda members" (Katzman and Thomas, 2017: 6).

This opening salvo of the war on terror was not brief; US troops withdrew from Afghanistan in late 2021, making it the longest war in US history. The Congressional appropriations and spending on the conflict from 2001 to 2021 are estimated to exceed $2.2 trillion (in current dollars). This figure does not include future interest payments or the future costs of veteran care (Watson Institute, 2021). An estimated 241,000 people have died as a direct consequence of the war, not including individuals who have died as an indirect result of the conflict (e.g., from disease, lack of access to food and medical care, etc.)

(Watson Institute, 2021). A full account of the failures in Afghanistan is beyond the scope of this section (for a more comprehensive discussion, see Horton, 2017). One aspect of US operations, however, clearly illustrates a number of relevant problems.

Throughout the last two decades, the United States has undertaken a series of policies in the country aimed at combating the Afghan drug trade, viewing such activities as a necessary condition for success in fighting global terrorism. This entanglement of counterdrug and counterterrorism policy is a particularly salient example of US policy failures and highlights both the knowledge constraints faced by policymakers and a number of perverse incentives.

In the 1970s, countries like Turkey, Iran, and Pakistan issued bans on the production of opium poppy – the plant from which opium and heroin, for example, are derived. By the end of that decade, many Afghan farmers began cultivating opium poppy; by 1989, opium was one of the country's leading exports (Cooley, 1999: 131). When the Taliban took control of the country in the mid-1990s, it is estimated that the group received some $30 million per year from the opium trade (Goodhand, 2005: 199). This changed, however, in 2000 when the Taliban issued a religious decree, or *fatwa*, banning the production of opium. The result was a sharp decline in poppy cultivation.

In the nearly twenty years since the launch of Operation Enduring Freedom, the US government has pursued several different policies related to opium production in Afghanistan. During the initial military campaign, for example, US forces largely ignored opium production in exchange for cooperation from local warlords (see Berniker, 2002). Following a spike in poppy production, the United States changed its stance on drugs in the country, undertaking an intensive campaign to abolish the poppy industry entirely. In December 2004, the United States' top commander in Afghanistan, Lieutenant General David W. Barno, stated that poppy eradication was necessary in order to win the war on terror, citing that drug interdiction would reduce the budgetary capabilities of terror groups (Felbab-Brown, 2009: 141). To this end, the State Department dedicated some $930 million to international drug eradication efforts (see Tarnoff, 2012). The DOD more than tripled its counternarcotics budget to in excess of $225 million.

The results were not what policymakers had expected. Despite a record amount of poppy being eradicated, Afghanistan logged a record poppy crop in 2006 (165,000 hectares) and the country became the world's largest opium producer – providing some 80 percent of the global supply of opium (United Nations Office on Drugs and Crime, 2014: 21). Beginning with the Obama administration in 2009, US officials switched policies in Afghanistan yet again. Though still viewing poppy eradication as a necessary component of the war on terror, policymakers employed a new strategy for fighting the drug trade. In an example of the "opportunity cost" approach to combating terrorism, the US government sought to move Afghan citizens away from opium production by providing them with "alternative livelihoods." Hundreds of programs have been attempted in Afghanistan, with some offering direct income transfers to individuals, and others offering assistance with growing other crops in exchange for signing a "poppy clause," agreeing to stop growing opium poppy (see Mansfield, 2020 for a detailed discussion). Like the policies that preceded it, this policy also failed. Speaking in 2014, the special inspector general for Afghan reconstruction said: "Afghan farmers are growing more opium today than at any time in their modern history" (Sopko, 2014: 2). In 2021, the United Nations reported that, as of 2019, "[t]he gross income from opiates exceeded the value of [Afghanistan's] officially recorded licit exports" (United Nations Office on Drugs and Crime, 2021: 5).

In addition to failing to reduce or eliminate the drug trade, the entanglement of counternarcotics operations in Afghanistan with counterterrorism operations generated a variety of unintended consequences, each of which effectively undermined US policy goals (see Coyne, Hall, and Burns, 2016). In reviewing these consequences, we again observe the limits of the knowledge available to policymakers and gain an appreciation for the incentives facing a variety of actors within and outside of government.

The first unintended consequence of this policy was the creation of "regime uncertainty" in Afghanistan. This refers to uncertainty regarding the future activities and policies of government. The citizens of Afghanistan, having witnessed multiple (radically different) policies related to the opium trade, could not be sure what policies the United States would pursue in the future. This not only meant that Afghans were less likely to accept US policies but undermined the credibility of both the US and the Afghan governments. This directly undercut the United States' goal of establishing a strong central government in Kabul.

The second unintended consequence of these policies relates to cartelization in the drug trade. Through the attempted disruption and elimination of opium production in Afghanistan, officials sought to target a major income source for terror groups. While these policies did remove some opium producers from the market, these changes did not produce the desired effects. Instead of disrupting or eliminating large-scale opium producers, these policies primarily impacted smaller producers. This occurred for two reasons. First, smaller operations were easier for officials to target. Second, many small producers self-selected to exit the market as they were unwilling to take on the additional risks of operating in the now-targeted opium market (i.e., they were unwilling to risk fines, prison, death, etc.). Those producers who remained in the market were the larger opium suppliers. These producers became increasingly intertwined with the Taliban, who offered these suppliers protection from US eradication efforts. Far from eliminating a primary income source for the Taliban, these policies had precisely the *opposite* effect. According to the United Nations, Afghanistan produced some 84 percent of the world's opium in 2019 (United Nations Office on Drugs and Crime, 2020: 9). Rather than forcing the group to tighten its purse strings, the policy had the effect of exploding the Taliban's budget to more than $1 billion. An estimated $416 million comes from the opium trade (Sufizada, 2020).

A third unintended consequence is that US efforts to eradicate the drug trade in Afghanistan effectively criminalized a large segment of the civilian population. Faced with the choice of economic destitution or aligning themselves with the Taliban (and receiving their protection from US interdiction policies), many Afghans chose the latter. With segments of the civilian population relying on the Taliban to protect their livelihoods, this undercut counterterrorism efforts as civilians became unwilling to work with US forces against the group. Moreover, this furthered the difficulties in establishing a stable central government in Kabul.

Of course, it was not just civilians who became entangled in the opium trade. The US government's making poppy cultivation illegal and engaging in intensive eradication efforts gave the Taliban and others strong incentives to evade drug policies. This led to rampant corruption among the political leadership in Afghanistan, many of whom willingly accepted bribes in exchange for overlooking narcotics activity. Other political leaders looked the other way after direct threats of violence, either against themselves or against their family members. Speaking on the extent of the corruption in the country, former special ambassador to Afghanistan Thomas Schweich stated: "Narco-traffickers were buying off hundreds of police chiefs, judges, and other officials. Narco-corruption went to the top of the Afghan government . . . . [The attorney general of Afghanistan] told me . . . that President Karzai . . . had directed him, for political reasons, not to prosecute any of these people" (Schweich, 2006: n.p.). This corruption further contributed to the difficulties of establishing a stable government in Afghanistan. It also complicated efforts to weaken the Taliban, who now had police officers, judges, and other government officials on its payroll.

These discussions of Libya and Afghanistan are but two of many examples of how US foreign policy in the war on terror has generated serious adverse consequences. It would be incorrect, however, to assume that the effects of the war on terror are limited to the international arena. In fact, some of the most profound effects of US counterterrorism policy are observable domestically. As discussed in Section 4, the 9/11 terror attacks and the subsequent war on terror may be thought of as a critical episode in the growth of government. The attacks on the World Trade Center and the Pentagon represented a crisis whereafter citizens called upon the government to "do something" to combat the terror threat. The war on terror was the answer to that call; so began a massive ratcheting up of domestic counterterrorism activities.

### Implications of the War on Terror: Domestic Effects

The war on terror is profoundly different from other, more traditional wars like World War II or the Vietnam War. While the war on terror does have external enemies (e.g., the Taliban and IS), there are domestic adversaries of the war as well. These "homegrown terrorists" are not readily identifiable. As a result, officials have looked to turn the tools of foreign intervention inward in the name of combating domestic terrorism. While this would appear to fit into the framework whereby policymakers maximize social welfare by trading off liberty for security, we observe in many cases how these tools not only diminish freedoms but fail to provide enhanced security. In some instances, safety is demonstrably *worse* as the implemented policies weaken constraints upon government actors or generate other unintended consequences.

Consider the broad and sweeping changes related to domestic surveillance policies. Although the US government's domestic surveillance apparatus can trace its origins to the beginning of the last century, the war on terror provided a clear opportunity for government officials to further grow the state's surveillance powers (see Coyne and Hall, 2018: 71–95). The PATRIOT Act, for instance, markedly expanded domestic surveillance capabilities in several ways. Section 213 of the PATRIOT Act allowed government officials to search private property without informing the owner (H.R. 3162, 2001: § 213). Section 214 weakened Fourth Amendment protections against unlawful search and seizure by making it easier for officials to conduct "tap and trace" searches that capture information related to incoming and outgoing phone calls (H.R. 3162, 2001: § 214). The following section, section 215, allowed the government to acquire a secret court order compelling third parties (e.g., phone companies or internet providers) to turn over "tangible things" in order to "protect against international terrorism" (H.R. 3162, 2001: § 215). The PATRIOT Act also expanded the ability of agencies like the FBI to issue "national security letters" (NSLs) – administrative subpoenas that allow government agents to access private data without judicial review (see Donohue, 2008).

In addition to the expansion in surveillance ushered in by the PATRIOT Act, other important changes occurred as well. For example, President Bush relaxed constraints on the NSA, allowing the agency to search the emails and phone calls of US citizens without first obtaining a warrant, in an effort to combat terrorism. These powers were further codified and expanded in 2008 (see Risen and Lichtblau, 2005; Lichtblau and Risen, 2009a, 2009b). In 2002, the *New York Times* reported that the DOD, along with the Defense Advanced Research Projects Agency (DARPA), was developing technology as part of a program titled "Total Information Awareness." The purpose of the program was to gather data about citizens to develop "information signatures" that officials could use to recognize and track *possible* terrorists or other criminals. The program would allow government agents to gather and use massive amounts of data about US citizens "without suspicion of wrongdoing or a warrant" (see Electronic Privacy Information Center, 2021).

Though the activities undertaken by the NSA, the FBI, and other agencies were intended to combat the threat of terrorism, it has since been revealed that many of them have not improved the safety and security of US citizens but *have* actively undermined civil liberties. In some cases, these actions have directly undermined US counterterrorism objectives. Beginning in June 2013, the *Washington Post* and the *Guardian* began publishing information provided by former NSA contractor Edward Snowden. The information supplied by Snowden illustrated to the broader public how the government's surveillance powers had expanded. He revealed, for example, that the government had pursued a mass collection of private phone records and that major US telecommunications companies had offered officials unlimited access to their customers' information. At least nine major tech companies, including Apple, Google, and Microsoft, received requests for data under a program called PRISM. The companies were not only required to comply with these requests but forced to keep it a secret. He revealed that the NSA had tapped into the data kept by Google and Yahoo! without their knowledge or consent, and that the Foreign Intelligence Surveillance Court (FISC) had issued orders allowing agencies like the CIA, the FBI, and the NSA to share information about US citizens.

In 2020, a full seven years after the Snowden revelations, a US Court of Appeals ruled in *United States* v. *Moalin* that US intelligence officials had been dishonest in their discussions of surveillance activities and that the mass collection of Americans' phone records was illegal, violating the Foreign Intelligence Surveillance Act (FISA) and possibly the US Constitution (see United States Court of Appeals for the Ninth Circuit, 2020: 3). Since the time the activities of the NSA were made public, officials had repeatedly asserted that their programming had been essential in foiling terror plots. They further pointed to the intelligence programs being integral in catching a Somali man, Basaaly Saeed Moalin, and three co-conspirators for collaborating to send funds to support a foreign terrorist organization. Writing for the court, Judge Marsha Berzon remarked that officials' claims that the information gathered by the intelligence programs had been vital to the case were not supported by the actual evidence.

> Having carefully reviewed the FISA applications and all related classified information, we are convinced that under established Fourth Amendment standards, the metadata collection, even if unconstitutional, did not taint the evidence introduced [e.g., was not essential in proving the guilt of the defendant] . . . . To the extent the public statements of government officials created a contrary impression, that impression is inconsistent with the contents of the classified records. (United States Court of Appeals for the Ninth Circuit, 2020: 23–24)

Discussing the Court's ruling, journalist Aaron Holmes highlighted the significance of the finding: "But the NSA could only point to one example [where the mass surveillance program had foiled terrorists] . . . [T]he appeals court ruled that not only was the collection of [the defendant's] records illegal, but *it was ultimately irrelevant to the conviction.* In other words, *there is zero evidence the NSA's phone-records program stopped a terrorist attack*" (Holmes, 2020: n.p., emphasis added).

This highlights a fundamental problem with the supposed liberty–security trade-off. Armed with the proper knowledge and well-aligned incentives, officials within the model select the optimal mix of security and liberty. Any reduction in liberty should correspond with an increase in safety and vice versa. The ruling from *Moalin*, however, illustrates but one case where the actions of officials undoubtedly reduced the civil liberties of citizens and violated US law but did not result in any increase in security. The intrusions into the lives of US citizens were not relevant in catching terrorists, despite what the officials stated. Though officials continue to claim that their programs have prevented acts of terrorism, they have provided no corroborating evidence. Taken together, this highlights that decreases in liberty can and do occur without any offsetting increase in safety.

Moreover, there is some evidence that the expansion of domestic surveillance and other counterterrorism policies have made Americans *less* safe on certain margins, as illustrated by the effects of the war on terror on US domestic police. Laws within the United States have attempted – with varying degrees of success – to separate the functions of the police and the military. The police are trained to act as peacekeepers and to uphold the rights of US citizens. These protections apply to both the victims and the perpetrators of crime. Violence is to be used only as a means of last resort. The military, by contrast, is trained to destroy external enemies, with violence an assumed requisite activity. The distinction between the police and the military has progressively eroded over time, with substantial changes occurring after the start of the war on drugs (see Hall and Coyne, 2013). The fear of terrorism in the post-9/11 era, however, created substantial room for the further integration of military tactics and equipment into police departments throughout the country as police found themselves on the "front lines" of the supposed terror threat. The result has been a progressively militarized police force, whereby police have adopted the attitudes, equipment, and tactics of the military (see Hall and Coyne, 2013; Coyne and Hall, 2016c, 2018).

Coyne and Yatsyshina (2021: 196) highlight how the expansion of domestic surveillance has critically affected local law enforcement: "Policing at the state and local levels has become increasingly intertwined with the surveillance state." One report from the Council of State Governments and Eastern Kentucky University (2006: 7) makes this point clearly.

> [S]tate law enforcement agencies are very involved in their states' homeland security initiatives . . . .. Approximately three-quarters of state law enforcement agencies report a great amount of involvement or serve as their state's leader for gathering, analyzing and sharing terrorism-related intelligence. Overall, state police are much more involved today than before Sept. 11 in building their state's intelligence capabilities, conducting terrorism-related investigations and coordinating and planning for homeland security.

As part of these operations, state and local police integrated a number of surveillance tools into their efforts – with limited or altogether absent oversight. Consider the use by law enforcement of cell-site simulators, otherwise known as "stingrays." Stingray technology allows for the user of the equipment to acquire data from cell phones, including location and other identifying information. Stingrays cannot distinguish between the cell phone of one individual and that of another, however. This means that the devices gather data from *all* the cell phones within a certain geographic area, meaning that innocent civilians are having their data collected and reviewed by law enforcement (see Zetter, 2020). The use of this technology is often subject to a nondisclosure agreement, allowing law enforcement agencies to be able to obtain and use the technology without offering any details about when, where, or how often they are used (see Glenza and Woolf, 2015)

In addition to these changes related to surveillance, the war on terror has engendered other transformations within domestic law enforcement. The 1033 and 1122 programs are clear illustrations. These programs allow for the transfer of military equipment, from protective vests and night-vision pieces to mine-resistant ambush-protected vehicles (MRAPs) and machine guns, to state and local police forces for use in their operations. The 1033 program saw unprecedented growth following the start of the war on terror. In 2010, the program transferred some $212 million in military equipment to law enforcement agencies. The following year, the number of equipment transfers totaled nearly $500 million (see Coyne and Hall, 2018: 113–115). It is evident that the continued integration of these tools, as well as other militaristic tactics like the use of Special Weapons and Tactics [SWAT] teams, has had serious negative consequences. Journalist Radley Balko has documented a variety of nefarious consequences of this militarization, including the deaths of innocent civilians (see Balko, 2014). Coyne and Hall highlight how this militarization has negatively impacted the civil liberties of particularly vulnerable communities, including prisoners and communities of color (see Coyne and Hall, 2016a, 2016b, 2018: 163–167).

Law enforcement, the military, and elected officials face strong incentives to continue this militarization process even if it is directly at odds with broader public welfare. The military is able to expand its power and the number of personnel under its purview by becoming increasingly intertwined with law enforcement. Local police are better able to acquire additional funding, staff, and equipment by linking their operations with those of federal authorities (see Hall and Coyne, 2013). Elected officials can claim to their constituents that they take a "tough" stance on issues like drugs, crime, and terrorism. Other agencies are likely to engage in these activities as well as seeking out opportunities to expand and become further integrated with the larger government. Goodman and Coyne (2022), for example, illustrate how American border security has become increasingly militarized, not out of necessity and for enhanced safety but because of astute political entrepreneurs.

Individuals may well expect that a government response to a terror attack would have implications for things like surveillance and policing. But the effects of the war on terror appear in other, wholly unexpected areas as well. Consider, for instance, recent discussions within the United States surrounding the issue of far-right extremism. Following the riot in Washington, DC, in which protestors (supporters of the outgoing president Donald Trump) breached the Capitol building, lawmakers, journalists, and the public renewed concerns about far-right extremism in the United States. It was revealed that a disproportionate number of those arrested had an explicit connection to the US military (see Sidner, Rappard, and Cohen, 2021).

In analyzing these linkages, Hall, Hassell, and Fitch (2021) argue that the connection between far-right domestic extremists and the military is directly tied to US policies associated with the war on terror. They detail how the need for additional military personnel led to a relaxation of military recruitment standards. This provided an avenue through which individuals with extremist views could more easily obtain military training and a way for extremist groups to recruit individuals with a military skillset. They illustrate how the number of violent events involving far-right extremists has increased since the start of the war on terror and point to several instances in which individuals used their military backgrounds to directly influence far-right extremist groups. The military wanted to recruit more people to carry out a variety of counterterrorism policies aimed at terrorists abroad, but one unintended consequence is that it provided groups aligned with far-right domestic terrorism additional human capital.

Though all the examples so far illustrate this idea, the connection between far-right extremism and the war on terror is a particularly salient example of the challenges encountered with the basic trade-off between liberty and security discussed in Section 4. Government action can reduce *both* liberty and safety (i.e., the curve shifts inward). Moreover, liberty and safety are not simple aggregate categories but instead consist of multiple, heterogenous margins. For instance, even *if* the relaxation of recruitment standards allowed the US military better to fight the war on terror abroad and increased safety in that way, the same policy may well have decreased safety by allowing for the growth in far-right extremism. Similarly, even if the acquisition of military equipment by police improved safety on some margins, it undoubtedly made individuals less safe on other margins, including by reducing civil liberties.

## Summing Up: Two Decades and Counting

As noted in Section 4, one of the factors that influences permanent expansion in the size of a government is the ideology of the citizenry, as well as those within the government. If individuals support the continued growth of government intervention, that intervention is likely to continue. The war on terror is no exception. The 9/11 attacks continue to exert profound influence over the attitudes of US citizens. One survey conducted in 2016 asked respondents to name the historic events in their lifetime that "have had the greatest impact on the country." Some three-quarters of those surveyed (76 percent) included 9/11 in their responses (Deane, Duggan, and Morin, 2016).

Support for some policies has waned. The majority of Americans surveyed (58 percent) approve of withdrawing from Afghanistan. Support for withdrawal is higher among Democrats and those in military households (see Frankovic, 2021). This is not to suggest that Americans no longer support the war on terror, however. As of early 2021, Americans still ranked terrorism as a "critical threat" to US vital interests. According to one poll, some 72 percent of those surveyed stated that international terrorism is a "critical" threat to the United States, while another 24 percent rated international terrorism as "important, not critical" (Brenan, 2021). Of those surveyed, 82 percent pointed to "cyberterrorism, the use of computers to cause disruption or fear in society," being a critical threat to the United States. A mere 2 percent of those surveyed stated that cyberterrorism is not an important threat (Brenan, 2021). The result of this fear is precisely what we would expect under the ratchet model. Nearly 115 pieces of legislation related to cybersecurity are currently under consideration by lawmakers. Many of these have strong bipartisan support (see Brumfield, 2021).

Support remains for other US counterterrorism policies as well. Half of Americans feel that the United States' defense spending is "about right" and some 62 percent report that US defense strength is "about right" (Jones, 2020). While some 75 percent of individuals surveyed in 2017 stated they would *not* give up their personal privacy with respect to email, internet, or phone records in order to help the US government thwart domestic terror plots, nearly 40 percent reported that US intelligence agencies are conducting "as much as necessary" or "not enough" surveillance on US citizens (see Volz, 2017). Taken together, this would suggest that the war on terror is likely to continue well into the future – with support from a broad segment of US citizens.

There will also be ongoing domestic effects. Following the riot at the US Capitol building in January 2021, the Biden administration announced major changes to domestic terrorism policing. Speaking to reporters, White House press secretary Jen Psaki stated: "The tragic deaths and destruction that occurred underscored what we have long known – the rise of domestic violent extremism is a serious and growing national security threat" (Psaki, 2021: n.p.). The secretary went on to discuss a three-part plan for combating extremism, including a "comprehensive threat assessment," the building of capabilities to combat domestic extremism, as well as the "coordinating [of] relevant parts of the federal government to enhance and accelerate efforts to address DVE [domestic violent extremism]" (Psaki, 2021: n.p.). Though the details of how the federal government plans to act are not specified, her address made clear that the administration intends its policies to be wide-reaching: "This ... process will focus on evolving threats, radicalization, the role of social media, and opportunities to improve information sharing, operation responses, and more" (Psaki, 2021: n.p.). The implementation of these programs, as well as future counterterrorism initiatives, will undoubtedly engender domestic consequences just as we have observed in the last two decades.

## 6 Conclusion

There are numerous areas that are ripe for additional research related to terrorism and counterterrorism. One area for future study is how societies might deal with the problem of "threat inflation," which is common among government policymakers. For instance, the role of threat inflation has been emphasized in the US government's framing of terrorism (Mueller, 2006; Mueller and Stewart, 2011, 2018, 2021) and in its response through the war on terror (Thrall and Cramer, 2009). Government officials often have an incentive to inflate threats in order to expand the scope and scale of their power. Threat inflation is problematic because it creates unnecessary fear among the domestic populace. In addition to the immediate psychological effects it has, fear is a pathway to permanent expansions in government power at the expense of private liberty. Given the incentives inherent in government, thinking about mechanisms to mitigate threat inflation is central to preventing opportunism by political actors.

A broader issue in constitutional political economy is how liberal societies can effectively navigate emergency situations. As Hayek (1979: 124) notes, emergencies often serve as the pretexts for permanent expansions in government and the erosion of constitutional constraints protecting the person and property of people living under the government. Along similar lines, Higgs (1987) documents how crisis situations lead to permanent expansions in the overall size of governments per the ratchet effect discussed in Section 4. This raises a fundamental tension related to constitutions – it is often argued that during times of crisis governments need "extra constitutional" powers, in the form of discretion and the use of force, to effectively deal with the emergency; yet it is precisely at these moments that governments are most likely to abuse their powers while establishing new precedents for future uses of power.

One solution to this "paradox of power" is to separate powers. Multiple mechanisms have been proposed, including separating powers within the government, which, in principle, would create a system of checks and balances against abuses of power and overreach. Another proposal is moving from a monocentric system to a polycentric system. A monocentric system is defined by a single decision-making unit. A polycentric system, in contrast, is one where there are numerous decision-making units with individual autonomy, operating within a common set of overarching rules. A polycentric system, relative to a monocentric system, offers several potential benefits (Coyne, 2020b: 230–231). These include allowing for the leveraging of local knowledge, enabling contestation and experimentation, better satisfying a diversity of preferences, dispersing risk because there is no single point of failure, and dispersing power. In addition to offering a potential way of constraining government, polycentric systems matter for treatments of terrorism.

Frey and Luechinger (2004) argue that decentralized decision-making may serve as a disincentive for terrorism. They note that most treatments of counterterrorism focus on disincentivizing terrorism by raising the cost of these behaviors. An alternative approach is to reduce the benefits of terrorist activity through decentralization. Numerous decision-making units would mean that the damage caused to a single unit would not destabilize the entire system because other units would remain in operation. That is, a decentralized system is more robust in the face of exogenous shocks, compared to a more centralized system. Scholars have combined insights from Austrian economics and public choice economics to study public administration and the governance of a free society (see Boettke, 2018; Aligica, Boettke, and Tarko, 2019).

Polycentric structures might also be a way of resolving the issue of threat inflation raised earlier. In matters of national security, democratic governments typically receive advice from a small group of security experts. Existing scholarship focuses on the factors leading to "expert failure" and how these can lead to ineffective, and harmful, policies (Levy and Peart, 2017; Koppl, 2018). One of the key conditions that makes expert failure more likely is the monopolization of expert decision-making. By preventing competition over ideas and alternative courses of action, this monopolization of expertise makes error more likely because of the fallibility and limited reason of any one person, or small group of people. In matters of national security in the United States, and in other countries, information is highly centralized and secret, while expert decision-making is monopolized by a small group of political elites (see Coyne, Goodman, and Hall, 2019). Polycentric systems can mitigate expert failure, and bad policy, by allowing for the contestation of ideas and experimentation with different ways of addressing social challenges, including terrorism and security (see Coyne and Goodman, 2020; Coyne, 2022).

A final topic for further study focuses on the connection between liberalism and terrorism (Boettke and Coyne, 2007). As discussed in Section 4, liberal societies face unique dilemmas when it comes to counterterrorism. At the same time, liberal societies are in a privileged position in terms of being able to contribute to actions that might reduce the underlying causes of the demand for terrorism. Liberal values include the primacy of individual freedom, respect for human dignity, intellectual humility, skepticism regarding rule by experts, and appreciation for voluntary choice and association, freedom of expression, economic freedom, toleration, pluralism, cosmopolitanism, spontaneous orders, and a commitment to peaceful solutions to interpersonal conflict. Institutions grounded in these values can help mitigate terrorism by offering people pathways that do not rely on violence through which to navigate tensions and conflicts.

Societies can take steps to foster liberal values both domestically and internationally. But what factors lead to the emergence and spread of liberal values within a society (McCloskey, 2019; McCloskey and Carden, 2020)? What factors lead to the erosion of liberal values once they are established? What is the relationship between market and morality within a society as it affects the core liberal values (see Storr and Choi, 2019)? These and similar questions are all opportunities for further study.

Internationally, societies can choose to elevate military force as a means of engaging others, or they can emphasize diplomacy, complacency, and appeasement to minimize the chance of conflict (Mueller, 2021; Coyne, 2022). Societies can also adjust their trade and migration policies to allow for the possibility of peaceful exchange across borders. This does not require intervening in other societies or attempting to impose institutions on them by force. Instead, it offers a pathway to peace if others choose to accept it. This raises a number of questions for future scholarship. What is the relationship between the "capitalist peace" associated with international trade and terrorism? How might markets create a "social space" (Storr, 2008) across borders to foster relationships that contribute to the peaceful resolution of conflict? What is the relationship among economic nationalism, protectionism, and terrorism?

Exploring the answers to these, and related, questions is crucial to understanding how terrorism can be reduced. As we have argued throughout this Element, permanently reducing the demand for terrorism requires changing the underlying conditions (i.e., shifting the demand curve inward). Counterterrorism policies might reduce the quantity demanded (i.e., movement along a given demand curve) at a given point in time, but they do not remove the underlying preferences driving demand. While not a panacea – terrorism has always been with us and always will be in some form or another – liberal institutions provide a way to mitigate the underlying, deep factors that contribute to the demand for terrorism.

# References

Abadie, A. (2006). Poverty, political freedom, and the roots of terrorism. *American Economic Review*, **96**(2), 50–56.

Abrahms, M. (2008). What terrorists really want: terrorist motives and counter-terrorism strategy. *International Security*, **32**(4), 78–105.

Ackerman, G., Abhayaratne, P., Bale, J. et al. (2006). *Assessing Terrorist Motivations for Attacking Critical Infrastructure*. Report No. UCRL-TR-227068. Livermore, CA: Lawrence Livermore National Lab. https://doi.org/10.2172/902328.

Alchian, A. A., and Allen, W. R. (1983). *Exchange and Production: Competition, Coordination, and Control*. Belmont, CA: Wadsworth.

Aligica, P. D. (2015). Addressing limits to mainstream economic activity of voluntary and nonprofit organizations: the "Austrian" alternative. *Nonprofit and Voluntary Sector Quarterly*, **44**(5), 1026–1040.

Aligica, P. D. (2018). *Public Entrepreneurship, Citizenship, and Self-Governance*. Cambridge: Cambridge University Press.

Aligica, P. D., Boettke, P. J., and Tarko, V. (2019). *Public Governance and the Classical-Liberal Perspective*. New York: Oxford University Press.

Al-Salhy, S., and Arango, T. (2014). "Sunni militants drive Iraqi army out of Mosul." *New York Times*, June 10. www.nytimes.com/2014/06/11/world/middleeast/militants-in-mosul.html.

Anderton, C. H., and Carter, J. R. (2005). On rational choice theory and the study of terrorism. *Defence and Peace Economics*, **16**(4), 275–282.

Anderton, C. H., and Carter, J. R. (2006). Applying intermediate microeconomics to terrorism. *Journal of Economic Education*, **37**(4), 442–458.

Balko, R. (2014). *Rise of the Warrior Cop: The Militarization of America's Police Forces*. New York: Public Affairs.

Basuchdoudhary, A., and Shughart, W. F. (2010). On ethnic conflict and the origins of transnational terrorism. *Defence and Peace Economics*, **21**(1), 65–87.

Beccaro, A. (2020). ISIS in Libya and beyond, 2014–2016.*Journal of North African Studies*, **27**(1), 160–179.

Bennett, J. T. (2017). *Homeland Security Scams*. New Brunswick, NJ: Transaction Publishers.

Bergen, P. N. D. (n.d.). "September 11 attacks." *Encyclopedia Britannica*. https://bit.ly/3LHMCPj.

Berman, E. (2003). Hamas, Taliban, and the Jewish underground: an economist's view of radical religious militias. NBER Working Paper No. 10004. www.nber.org/papers/w10004.

Berman, E., and Iannaccone, L. R. (2006). Religious extremism: the good, the bad, and the deadly. *Public Choice*, **128**(1), 109–129.

Berman, E., and Laitin, D. (2005). Hard targets: theory and evidence on the tactical use of suicide attacks. NBER Working Paper No. 11740. www .nber.org/papers/w11740.

Berniker, M. (2002). "Afghanistan: back to bad opium habits." *Asia Times*, December 25. www.latimes.com/atimes/Central_Asia/DL25Ag01.html.

Bhui, K., James, A., and Wessely, S. (2016). Mental illness and terrorism. *British Medical Journal*, **354**(i4869), 1–2.

Boettke, P. J. (2018). Economics and public administration. *Southern Economic Journal*, **84**(4), 938–959.

Boettke, P. J. (2021). *The Struggle for a Better World*. Arlington, VA: Mercatus Center at George Mason University.

Boettke, P. J., and Coyne, C. J. (2007). Liberalism in the post-9/11 world. *Indian Journal of Economics & Business*, Special Issue, 35–53.

Boettke, P. J., Coyne, C. J., and Leeson, P. T. (2008). Institutional stickiness and the new development economics. *American Journal of Economics and Sociology*, **67**(2), 331–358.

Boettke, P. J., and Prychitko, D. L. (2004). Is an independent nonprofit sector prone to failure? Toward an Austrian school interpretation of nonprofit and voluntary action. *Conversations on Philanthropy*, **1**, 1–40.

Boettke, P. J., and Storr, V. H. (2002). Post-classical political economy: polity, society and economy in Weber, Mises, and Hayek. *American Journal of Economics and Sociology*, **61**(1), 161–191.

Bohanon, C., and Van Cott, T. N. (2002). Now more than ever, your vote doesn't matter. *Independent Review*, **6**(4), 591–595.

Boudreaux, D. J. (1996). Was your high school civics teacher right after all? Donald Wittman's *The Myth of Democratic Failure. Independent Review*, **1**(1), 111–128.

Brenan, M. (2021). "Cyberterrorism tops list of 11 potential threats to the U.S." *Gallup*, March 22. https://bit.ly/3Hp95hc.

Brennan, J. (2016). *Against Democracy*. Princeton, NJ: Princeton University Press.

Brumfield, C. (2021). "US Congress tees up ambitious cybersecurity agenda in the wake of supply chain, ransomware attacks." *CSO*, June 14. https://bit.ly/3Hr1OgZ.

Buchanan, J. M. (1949). The pure theory of government finance. *Journal of Political Economy*, **57**(6), 496–505.

Buchanan, J. M. (1954). Social choice, democracy, and free markets. *Journal of Political Economy*, **62**(2), 114–123.

Buchanan, J. M. (1959). Positive economics, welfare economics, and political economy. *Journal of Law and Economics*, **2**, 124–138.

Buchanan, J. M. (1969). *Cost and Choice: An Inquiry Into Economic Theory.* Chicago, IL: University of Chicago Press.

Buchanan, J. M. (1979). Natural and artificial man. In *What Should Economists Do?* Indianapolis, IN: Liberty Fund Books, pp. 93–114.

Bueno de Mesquita, E. (2008). The political economy of terrorism: a selective overview of recent work. *Political Economist*, **10**(1), 1–12.

Bush, G. W. (2001a). "Remarks by the President upon arrival: the South Lawn." September 16. https://bit.ly/3oO4krb.

Bush, G. W. (2001b). "Address to a joint session of [the 107th] Congress and the American people." September 20. https://bit.ly/3ngukeu.

Capellan, J. A. (2015). Lone wolf terrorist or deranged shooter? A study of ideological active shooter events in the United States, 1970–2014. *Studies in Conflict & Terrorism*, **38**(6), 395–413.

Caplan, B. (2006). Terrorism: The relevance of the rational choice model. *Public Choice*, **128**(1–2), 91–107.

Chaliand, G., and Blin, A. (eds.). (2016). *The History of Terrorism: From Antiquity to ISIS*. Oakland: University of California Press.

Chamlee-Wright, E. (2010). *The Cultural and Political Economy of Recovery: Social Learning in a Post-Disaster Environment*. New York: Routledge.

Chamlee-Wright, E., and Myers, J. A. (2008). Discovery and social learning in non-priced environments: an Austrian view of social network theory. *Review of Austrian Economics*, **21**(2), 151–166.

Chenoweth, E. (2010). Democratic pieces: democratization and the origins of terrorism. In R. Reuveny and W. R. Thompson (eds.) *Coping with Terrorism: Origins, Escalation, Counterstrategies, and Responses*. Albany: State University of New York Press, pp. 97–123.

Chenoweth, E. (2013). Terrorism and democracy. *Annual Review of Political Science*, **16**, 355–378.

Coggins, B. L. (2015). Does state failure cause terrorism? An empirical analysis (1999–2008). *Journal of Conflict Resolution*, **59**(3), 455–483.

Cooley, J. (1999). *Unholy Wars: Afghanistan, American, and International Terrorism*. London: Pluto Press.

Cordesman, A. H., Loi, C., and Kocharlakota, V. (2010). "IED metrics for Iraq: June 2003–September 2010." *Center for Strategic and International Studies*, November 11. www.csis.org/analysis/afghan-and-iraqi-metrics-and-ied-threat.

Corwin, E. S. (1947). *Total War and the Constitution*. New York: Alfred Knopf.

Council of State Governments, and Eastern Kentucky University. (2006). "The impact of terrorism on state law enforcement: adjusting to new roles and changing conditions." December. www.ncjrs.gov/pdffiles1/nij/grants/216642.pdf.

Coyne, C. J. (2008). *After War: The Political Economy of Exporting Democracy*. Stanford, CA: Stanford University Press.

Coyne, C. J. (2013). *Doing Bad by Doing Good: Why Humanitarian Action Fails*. Stanford, CA: Stanford University Press.

Coyne, C. J. (2015). Lobotomizing the defense brain. *Review of Austrian Economics*, **28**(4), 371–396.

Coyne, C. J. (2018). The protective state. In P. J. Boettke and S. Stein (eds.) *Buchanan's Tensions: Reexamining the Political Economy and Philosophy of James M. Buchanan*. Arlington, VA: Mercatus Center at George Mason University, pp. 149–169.

Coyne, C. J. (2020a). *Defense, Peace, and War Economics* (Elements in Austrian Economics). Cambridge: Cambridge University Press.

Coyne, C. J. (2020b). Introduction: symposium on polycentric systems in a free society. *Independent Review*, **25**(2), 229–233.

Coyne, C. J. (2021). Introduction: symposium on the war on terror at twenty. *Independent Review*, **26**(2), 165–172.

Coyne, C. J. (2022). *In Search of Monsters to Destroy: The Folly of American Empire and the Paths to Peace*. Oakland, CA: Independent Institute.

Coyne, C. J., and Boettke, P. J. (2009). The problem of credible commitment in reconstruction. *Journal of Institutional Economics*, **5**(1), 1–23.

Coyne, C. J., and Bradley, A. R. (2019). Ludwig von Mises on war and the economy. *Review of Austrian Economics*, **32**(3), 215–228.

Coyne, C. J., and Goodman, N. P. (2020). Polycentric defense. *Independent Review*, **25**(2), 279–292.

Coyne, C. J., Goodman, N. P., and Hall, A. R. (2019). Sounding the alarm: the political economy of whistleblowing in the US security state. *Peace Economics, Peace Science, and Public Policy*, **25**(1), 1–11.

Coyne, C. J., and Hall, A. R. (2016a). Empire state of mind: the illiberal foundations of liberal hegemony. *Independent Review*, **21**(2), 237–250.

Coyne, C. J., and Hall, A. R. (2016b). Foreign intervention, police militarization, and minorities. *Peace Review: A Journal of Social Justice*, **28**(2), 165–170.

Coyne, C. J., and Hall, A. R. (2016c). Perfecting tyranny: foreign intervention and experimentation in state control. *Independent Review*, **19**(2), 165–189.

Coyne, C. J., and Hall, A. R. (2018). *Tyranny Comes Home: The Domestic Fate of U.S. Militarism*. Stanford, CA: Stanford University Press.

Coyne, C. J., and Hall, A. R. (2019). State-provided defense as non-comprehensive planning. *Journal of Private Enterprise*, **34**(1), 75–109.

Coyne, C. J., and Hall, A. R. (2021). *Manufacturing Materialism: U.S. Government Propaganda in the War on Terror*. Stanford, CA: Stanford University Press.

Coyne, C. J., Hall, A. R., and Burns, S. (2016). The war on drugs in Afghanistan: another failed experiment with interdiction. *Independent Review*, **21**(1), 95–119.

Coyne, C. J., and Lucas, D. S. (2016). Economists have no defense: a critical review of national defense in economics textbooks. *Journal of Private Enterprise*, **31**(4), 65–83.

Coyne, C. J., and Mathers, R. L. (2010). The fatal conceit of foreign intervention. *Advances in Austrian Economics*, **14**, 227–252.

Coyne, C. J., and Pellillo, A. (2011). Economic reconstruction amidst conflict: insights from Afghanistan and Iraq. *Defence and Peace Economics*, **22**(6), 627–643.

Coyne, C. J., and Yatsyshina, Y. (2021). Police state, U.S.A. *Independent Review*, **26**(2), 189–204.

Crenshaw, M. (1981). The causes of terrorism. *Comparative Politics*, **14**(4), 379–399.

Crenshaw, M. (1995). Introduction. In M. Crenshaw (ed.) *Terrorism in Context*. University Park: Pennsylvania State University Press, pp. 3–24.

Deane, C., Duggan, M., and Morin, R. (2016). "Americans name the 10 most significant historic events of their lifetimes." *Pew Research Center*, December 15. https://bit.ly/3NwhWBA.

De la Calle, L., and Sánchez-Cuenca, I. (2012). Rebels without a territory: an analysis of nonterritorial conflicts in the world, 1970–1997. *Journal of Conflict Resolution*, **56**(4), 580–603.

DiLorenzo, T. J. (1990). The subjectivist roots of James Buchanan's economics. *Review of Austrian Economics*, **4**, 180–195.

Donohue, L. K. (2008). *The Cost of Counterterrorism: Power, Politics, and Liberty*. New York: Cambridge University Press.

Dorsen, N. (1989). Foreign affairs and civil liberties. *American Journal of International Law*, **83**(4), 840–850.

Downs, Anthony. (1957). *An Economic Theory of Democracy*. New York: Harper.

Duncan, T. K., and Coyne, C. J. (2013a). The overlooked costs of the permanent war economy: a market process approach. *Review of Austrian Economics*, **26**(4), 413–431.

Duncan, T. K., and Coyne, C. J. (2013b). The origins of the permanent war economy. *Independent Review*, **18**(2), 219–240.

Duncan, T. K., and Coyne, C. J. (2015). The political economy of foreign intervention. In P. J. Boettke and C. J. Coyne (eds.) *The Oxford Handbook of Austrian Economics*. New York: Oxford University Press, pp. 678–697.

Electronic Privacy Information Center. (2021). "~~Total~~ 'Terrorism' Information Awareness (TIA)." https://epic.org/privacy/profiling/tia/#introduction.

El Taraboulsi-McCarthy, S., Al-Bayati, G., Metcalfe-Hough, V., and Adamczyk, S. (2019). Protection of displaced Libyans. Humanitarian Policy Group Working Paper. https://odi.org/en/publications/protection-of-displaced-libyans-risks-responses-and-border-dynamics/.

Enders, W., and Sandler, T. (2000). Is transnational terrorism becoming more threatening? A time-series investigation. *Journal of Conflict Resolution*, **44**(3), 307–332.

Enders, W., and Sandler, T. (2004). What do we know about the substitution effect in transnational terrorism? In A. Silke (eds.) *Research on Terrorism*. London: Routledge, pp. 119–137.

Enders, W., and Sandler, T. (2012). *The Political Economy of Terrorism*. New York: Cambridge University Press.

Eubank, W. L., and Weinberg, L. (1994). Does democracy encourage terrorism? *Terrorism and Political Violence*, **6**(4), 417–435.

Executive Order 13228. (2001). "Establishing the Office of Homeland Security and the Homeland Security Council." *Federal Register: The Daily Journal of the United States Government*. October 8. https://bit.ly/3HkhzGD.

Eyerman, J. (1998). Terrorism and democratic states: soft targets or accessible systems. *International Interactions*, **24**(2), 151–170.

Fair, E. (2016). *Consequence: A Memoir*. New York: Henry Holt & Company.

Fallon, M. (2017). *Unjustifiable Means: The Inside Story of How the CIA, Pentagon, and US Government Conspired to Torture*. New York: Regan Arts.

Fawaz, G. A. (2016). *ISIS: A History*. Princeton, NJ: Princeton University Press.

Fearon, J. D., and Laitin, D. D. (1996). Explaining interethnic cooperation. *American Political Science Review*, **90**(4), 715–735.

Felbab-Brown, V. (2009). *Shooting Up: Counterinsurgency and the War on Drugs*. Washington, DC: Brookings Institute Press.

Fishstein, P., and Wilder, A. (2012). "Winning hearts and minds? Examining the relationship between aid and security." *Tufts Security: Feinstein International Center*. https://bit.ly/42391eY.

Foreign Broadcast Information Service. (2004). "Compilation of Usama Bin Ladin statements: 1994–January 2004." https://irp.fas.org/world/para/ubl-fbis.pdf.

Fraenkel, O. K. (1946). War, civil liberties, and the supreme court. *Yale Law Journal*, **55**(4), 715–734.

Frankovic, K. (2021). "Americans support decision to withdraw U.S. force from Afghanistan." *YouGov America*, April 23. https://bit.ly/3LCZ9Dy.

Frey, B. (2004). *Dealing with Terrorism – Stick or Carrot?* Cheltenham: Edward Elgar.

Frey, B., and Luechinger, S. (2004). Decentralization as a disincentive for terrorism. *European Journal of Political Economy*, **20**(2), 509–515.

Fustos, K. (2011). "The Global Muslim Population." *Population Reference Bureau*, June 3. www.prb.org/resources/the-global-muslim-population/.

Gadarian, S. K. (2010). The politics of threat: how terrorism news shapes foreign policy attitudes. *Journal of Politics*, **72**(2), 469–483.

Gaibulloev, K., and Sandler, T. (2019). What we have learned about terrorism since 9/11. *Journal of Economic Literature*, **57**(2), 275–328.

Ganor, B. (2002). Defining terrorism: is one man's terrorist another man's freedom fighter? *Police Practice and Research*, **3**(4), 287–304.

Gates, R. (2014). "The quiet fury of Robert Gates." *Wall Street Journal*, January 7. www.wsj.com/articles/SB10001424052702304617404579306851526222552.

Gelman, A., Silver, N., and Edlin, A. (2012). What is the probability your vote will make a difference? *Economic Inquiry*, **50**(2), 321–326.

Gjoza, E. (2019). De-risking and the knowledge problem: the unseen consequences of financial sanctions. In S. Haeffele, A. R. Hall, and A. Millsap (eds.) *Informing Public Policy: Analyzing Contemporary U.S. and International Policy Issues Through the Lens of Market Process Economics*. New York: Rowman & Littlefield International, pp. 171–192.

Glennon, M. J. (2015). *National Security and Double Government*. New York: Oxford University Press.

Glenza, J., and Woolf, N. (2015). "Stingray spying: FBI's secret deal with police hides phone dragnet with courts." *Guardian*, April 10. https://bit.ly/3oTrCvW.

Global Terrorism Database. (2021). "Global Terrorism Database." University of Maryland National Consortium for the Study of Terrorism and Responses to Terrorism. https://bit.ly/44equmH.

Goepner, E. (2016). Measuring the effectiveness of America's war on terror. *US Army War College Quarterly: Parameters*, **46**(1), 107–120.

Goodhand, J. (2005). Frontiers and wars: the opium economy in Afghanistan. *Journal of Agrarian Change*, **5**(2), 191–216.

Goodman, N. P., and Coyne, C. J. (2022). U.S. border militarization and foreign policy: a symbiotic relationship. *Economics of Peace and Security Journal*, **17**(1), 5–16.

Hall, A. R., and Coyne, C. J. (2013). The militarization of U.S. domestic policy. *Independent Review*, **17**(4), 485–504.

Hall, A. R., Hassell, J. T., and Fitch, C. H. (2021). Militarized extremism: the radical right and the war on terror. *Independent Review*, **26**(2), 225–242.

Hammond, R. A., and Axelrod, R. (2006). The evolution of ethnocentrism. *Journal of Conflict Resolution*, **50**(6), 926–936.

Hampton, T. (2006). "Health effects from 9/11." *JAMA Network*, May 24. https://jamanetwork.com/journals/jama/fullarticle/202894.

Hassan, N. (2001). "An arsenal of believers: talking to the 'human bombs.'" *The New Yorker*, November 19. www.newyorker.com/magazine/2001/11/19/an-arsenal-of-believers.

Hayek, F. A. (1945). The use of knowledge in society. *American Economic Review*, **4**(35), 519–530.

Hayek, F. A. (1979). *The Political Order of a Free People*. Vol. III of *Law Legislation and Liberty*. Chicago, IL: University of Chicago Press.

Heckelman, J. C. (2003). Now more than ever, your vote doesn't count: a reconsideration. *Independent Review*, **7**(4), 599–601.

Henderson, D. (2016). An economist's case for a noninterventionist foreign policy. *Independent Review*, **21**(2), 199–217.

Higgs, R. (1987). *Crisis and Leviathan: Critical Episodes in the Growth of American Government*. New York: Oxford University Press.

Higgs, R. (2004). *Against Leviathan: Government Power and a Free Society*. Oakland, CA: Independent Institute.

Higgs, R. (2006). *Depression, War, and Cold War: Studies in Political Economy*. New York: Oxford University Press.

Higgs, R. (2007). *Neither Liberty nor Safety: Fear, Ideology, and the Growth of Government*. Oakland, CA: Independent Institute.

Higgs, R. (2008). The complex course of ideological change. *American Journal of Economics and Sociology*, **67**(4), 547–565.

Higgs, R. (2012). *Delusions of Power: New Explorations of the State, War, and the Economy*. Oakland, CA: Independent Institute.

Hoffman, B. (2017). *Inside Terrorism*. 3rd ed. New York: Columbia University Press.

Hoffman, B., and McCormick, G. (2004). Terrorism, signaling, and suicide attack. *Studies in Conflict and Terrorism*, **27**, 243–281.

Holmes, A. (2020). "The NSA phone-spying program exposed by Edward Snowden didn't stop a single terrorist attack, federal judge finds." *Insider*, September 2. www.businessinsider.com/nsa-phone-snooping-illegal-court-finds-2020-9.

Horton, S. (2017). *Fool's Errand: Time to End the War in Afghanistan*. Austin, TX: Libertarian Institute.

H.R. 3162. (2001). "Uniting and strengthening America by providing appropriate tools required to intercept and obstruct terrorism (USA PATRIOT ACT) act of 2001." www.congress.gov/bill/107th-congress/house-bill/3162.

Iannaccone, L. B. (2006). The market for martyrs. *International Journal of Research and Religion*, **2**(4), 1–28.

Institute for Economics and Peace. (2020). "Global terrorism index 2020: measuring the impact of terrorism." *Vision of Humanity*. Sydney, November. http://visionofhumanity.org/reports.

Johnson, J. (2016). "Statement by Secretary Jeh Johnson according first round of DHS's countering violent extremism grants." *U.S. Department of Homeland Security*, January 13. https://bit.ly/3Nna2uz.

Joint Chiefs of Staff. (2014). "Counterterrorism." Joint Publication 3-26, October 24. www.hsdl.org/?view&did=759133.

Jones, J. M. (2020). "Record high say U.S. defense spending is 'about right.'" *Gallup*, March 16. https://news.gallup.com/poll/288761/record-high-say-defense-spending-right.aspx.

Jordan, H. T., Osahan, S., Li, J. et al. (2019). Persistent mental and physical health impact of exposure to the September 11, 2001 world trade center terror attacks. *Environmental Health*, **18**(12), 1–16.

Karuri, K. (2016). "Obama: aftermath of Gaddafi overthrow, 'worst mistake as president.'" *Africa News*, November 4. https://bit.ly/3Hjdnac.

Katzman, K., and Thomas, C. (2017). "Afghanistan: post-Taliban governance, security, and U.S. policy." *Congressional Research Service*, December 13. https://sgp.fas.org/crs/row/RL30588.pdf.

Kennedy, R. (1999). Is one person's terrorist another's freedom fighter? Western and Islamic approaches to "just war" compared. *Terrorism and Political Violence*, **11**(1), 1–21.

Kenyon, J., Baker-Beall, C., and Binder, J. (2021). Lone-actor terrorism – a systematic literature review. *Studies in Conflict & Terrorism*. https://doi.org/10.1080/1057610X.2021.1892635.

Kirzner, I. M. (1973). *Competition and Entrepreneurship*. Chicago, IL: University of Chicago Press.

Kirzner, I. M. (1985). *Discover and the Capitalist Process*. Chicago, IL: University of Chicago Press.

Kirzner, I. M. (1997). Entrepreneurial discovery and the competitive market process. *Journal of Economic Literature*, **35**(1), 60–85.

Kirzner, I. M. (2000). *The Driving Force of the Market: Essays in Austrian Economics*. London: Routledge.

Koppl, R. (2018). *Expert Failure*. New York: Cambridge University Press.

Krieger, T., and Meierrieks, D. (2011). What causes terrorism? *Public Choice*, **147**, 3–27.

Krueger, A., and Malečková, J. (2003). Education, poverty and terrorism: is there a causal connection? *Journal of Economic Perspectives*, **17**(4), 119–144.

Kurrild-Klitgaard, P., Justesen, M. K., and Klemmensen, R. (2006). The political economy of freedom, democracy, and transnational terrorism. *Public Choice*, **128**(1), 289–315.

Kydd, A., and Walter, B. F. (2002). Sabotaging the peace: The politics of extremist violence. *International Organization*, **56**(2), 263–296.

Landes, W. M. (1978). An economic study of US aircraft hijackings, 1961–1976. *Journal of Law and Economics*, **2**(1), 1–31.

Laqueur, W. (1987). *The Age of Terrorism*. Boston, MA: Little, Brown & Company.

Laqueur, W. (1999). *The New Terrorism: Fanaticism and the Arms of Mass Destruction*. New York: Oxford University Press.

Larémont, R. R. (2013). After the fall of Qaddafi: political, economic, and security consequences for Libya, Mali, Niger, and Algeria. *Stability: International Journal of Security Development*, **2**(2), 1–8.

Law, R. D. (2009). *Terrorism: A History*. Cambridge: Polity Press.

Law, R. D. (ed.). (2015). *The Routledge History of Terrorism*. New York: Routledge.

Law, R. D. (2016). *Terrorism: A History*. 2nd ed. Cambridge: Polity Press.

Law, R. D. (2020). The evolution of terrorism: historical underpinnings and the development of group terrorism. In C. A. Ireland, M. Lewis, A. C. Lopez, and J. L. Ireland (eds.) *The Handbook of Collective Violence: Current Developments and Understanding*. Abingdon: Routledge, pp. 85–99.

Lee, A. (2011). Who becomes a terrorist? Poverty, education, and the origins of political violence. *World Politics*, **63**(2), 203–245a.

Levy, D. M., and Peart, S. J. (2017). *Escape from Democracy: The Role of Experts and the Public in Economic Policy*. New York: Cambridge University Press.

Lichbach, M. (1994). Rethinking rationality and rebellion: theories of collective action and problems of collective dissent. *Rationality and Society*, **6**(1), 8–39.

Lichbach, M. (1996). *The Cooperator's Dilemma*. Ann Arbor: University of Michigan Press.

Lichtblau, E., and Risen, J. (2009a). "Officials say U.S. wiretaps exceed law." *New York Times*, April 16. www.nytimes.com/2009/04/16/us/16nsa.html.

Lichtblau, E., and Risen, J. (2009b). "U.S. wiretapping of limited value, officials report." *New York Times*, July 10. www.nytimes.com/2009/07/11/us/11nsa.html.

Lum, C., Kennedy, L. W., and Sherley, A. (2006). Are counter-terrorism strategies effective? The results of the Campbell systematic review on counter-terrorism evaluation research. *Journal of Experimental Criminology*, **2**, 489–516.

Lutz, J. M., and Lutz, B. J. (2005). Definitions, classifications, and causes. In *Terrorism: Origins and Evolutions*. New York: Palgrave Macmillan, pp. 6–18.

Mansfield, D. (2020). Trying to be all things to all people: alternative development in Afghanistan. In J. Buxton, M. Chinery-Hesse, and K. Tinaste (eds.) *International Development Policy*, Vol. 12. Geneva: Geneva Graduate Institute.

McCartney, J., and McCartney, S. (2015). *America's War Machine: Vested Interests, Endless Conflict*. New York: Thomas Dunne Books.

McCloskey, D. N. (2019). *Why Liberalism Works: How True Liberal Values Produce a Freer, More Equal, Prosperous World for All*. New Haven, CT: Yale University Press.

McCloskey, D. N., and Carden, A. (2020). *Leave Me Alone and I'll Make You Rich: How the Bourgeois Deal Enriched the World*. Chicago, IL: University of Chicago Press.

McCoy, A. (2007). *A Question of Torture: CIA Interrogation, from the Cold War to the War on Terror*. New York: Henry Holt & Company.

Melman, S. (1970). *Pentagon Capitalism: The Political Economy of War*. New York: McGraw-Hill.

Melman, S. (1974). *The Permanent War Economy: American Capitalism in Decline*. New York: Simon & Schuster.

Mises, L. (1996). *Liberalism: The Classical Tradition*. Irvington-on-Hudson, NY: Foundation for Economic Education.

Mises, L. (1998). *Human Action: A Treatise on Economics*. Auburn, AL: Ludwig von Mises Institute.

Mueller, D. C. (2003). *Public Choice III*. Cambridge: Cambridge University Press.

Mueller, J. (2006). *Overblown: How Politicians and the Terrorism Industry Inflate National Security Threats, and Why We Believe Them*. New York: Free Press.

Mueller, J. (2021). *The Stupidity of War: American Foreign Policy and the Case for Complacency*. New York: Cambridge University Press.

Mueller, J., and Stewart, M. G. (2011). *Terror, Security, and Money: Balancing the Risks, Benefits, and Costs of Homeland Security*. New York: Oxford University Press.

Mueller, J., and Stewart, M. G. (2018). *Public Opinion and Counterterrorism Policy*. Washington, DC: Cato Institute. https://bit.ly/3Wndtnh.

Mueller, J., and Stewart, M. G. (2021). Terrorism and bathtubs: comparing and assessing the risk. *Terrorism and Political Violence*, **1**, 138–163.

Murtazashvili, I., and Murtazashvili, J. B. (2019). The political economy of state building. *Journal of Public Finance and Public Choice*, **34**(2), 189–207.

Murtazashvili, J. B. (2016). *Informal Order and the State in Afghanistan*. New York: Cambridge University Press.

Murtazashvili, J. B., and Murtazashvili, I. (2020). Wealth-destroying states. *Public Choice*, **182**(3), 353–371.

Murtazashvili, J. B., and Murtazashvili, I. (2021). *Land, the State, and War: Property Institutions and Political Order in Afghanistan*. New York: Cambridge University Press.

National Commission on Terrorist Attacks. (2004). *The 9/11 Commission Report: Final Report of the National Commission on Terrorist Attacks upon the United States*. Authorized ed. New York: W.W. Norton & Company.

Neily, C. (2021). "Are a disproportionate number of federal judges former government advocates?" CATO Institute. https://bit.ly/41OVVCq.

Niskanen, W. A. (1971). *Bureaucracy and Representative Government*. Chicago, IL: Aldine-Atherton.

Niskanen, W. A. (1975). Bureaucrats and politicians. *Journal of Law and Economics*, **18**(3), 617–643.

Niskanen, W. A. (2001). Bureaucracy. In W. F. Shughart II and L. Razzolini (eds.) *The Elgar Companion to Public Choice*. Cheltenham: Edward Elgar, pp. 258–270.

Oberschall, A. (2006). Explaining terrorism: the contribution of collective action theory. *Sociological Theory*, **22**(4), 26–37.

Olson, M. (1965). *The Logic of Collective Action: Public Goods and the Theory of Groups*. Cambridge, MA: Harvard University Press.

Palagashvili, L., Piano, E., and Skarbek, D. (2017). *The Decline and Rise of Institutions: A Modern Survey of the Austrian Contributions to the Economic Analysis of Institutions* (Elements in Austrian Economics). Cambridge: Cambridge University Press.

Pape, R. A. (2003). The strategic logic of suicide terrorism. *American Political Science Review*, **97**(3), 1–19.

Pape, R. A. (2005). *Dying to Win: The Strategic Logic of Suicide Terrorism*. New York: Random House.

Perl, R. (2007). "Combating terrorism: the challenge of measuring effectiveness." Congressional Research Service. https://sgp.fas.org/crs/terror/RL33160.pdf.

Piazza, J. A. (2013). Regime age and terrorism: are new democracies prone to terrorism? *International Interactions*, **39**(2), 246–263.

Posner, E. A., and Vermeule, A. (2007). *Terror in the Balance: Security, Liberty, and the Courts*. New York: Oxford University Press.

Prados, A. B., and Blanchard, C. M. (2004). "Saudi Arabia: terrorist financing issues." Congressional Research Service Report to Congress. https://fas.org/irp/crs/RL32499.pdf.

Priest, D., and Arkin, W. M. (2011). *Top Secret America: The Rise of the New American Security State*. New York: Little, Brown, & Company.

Psaki, J. (2021). "Press briefing by press secretary Jen Psaki and national economic director Brian Deese." White House, January 22. https://bit.ly/41KnUTO.

Public Law 107-40. (2001). "Authorization for use of military force." September 18. www.congress.gov/107/plaws/publ40/PLAW-107publ40.pdf.

Public Law 107-243. (2002). "Authorization for use of military force." October 16. www.congress.gov/107/plaws/publ243/PLAW-107publ243.pdf.

Rathbone, A., and Rowley, C. K. (2002). Terrorism. *Public Choice*, **111**(1–2), 9–18.

Rehnquist, W. H. (1998). *All the Laws but One: Civil Liberties in Wartime*. New York: Vintage Books.

Rejali, D. (2007). *Torture and Democracy*. Princeton, NJ: Princeton University Press.

Reksulak, M., Razzolini, L., and Shughart II, W. F. (2014). *The Elgar Companion to Public Choice*. 2nd ed. Northampton: Edward Elgar.

Risen, J., and Lichtblau, E. (2005). "Bush lets U.S. spy on callers without courts: secret order to widen domestic monitoring." *New York Times*, December 16. www.pulitzer.org/winners/james-risen-and-eric-lichtblau.

Ritchie, H., Hasell, J., Appel, C., and Roser, M. (2019). "Terrorism." Our World in Data. https://ourworldindata.org/terrorism.

Rossiter, C. (2009 [1948]). *Constitutional Dictatorship: Crisis Government in the Modern Democracies*. New Brunswick, NJ: Transaction Publishers.

Roth, J., Greenburg, D., and Wille, S. (n.d.). "Monograph on terrorist financing." National Commission on Terrorist Attacks Upon the United States. https://bit.ly/3NiPIKN.

Roos, D. (2020). "5 ways September 11 changed America." *History.com*, March 10. www.history.com/news/september-11-changes-america.

Rowley, C. K., and Schneider, F. (2004). *The Encyclopedia of Public Choice* (2 vols.). New York: Springer.

Sageman, M. (2008). How to study terrorism in the twenty-first century. In *Leaderless Jihad: Terror Networks in the Twenty-First Century*. Philadelphia: University of Pennsylvania Press, pp. 13–28.

Sandler, T. (2015). Terrorism and counterterrorism: an overview. *Oxford Economic Papers*, **67**(1), 1–20.

Sandler, T., and Enders, W. (2004). An economic perspective on transnational terrorism. *European Journal of Political Economy*, **20**(2), 301–316.

Savage, C. (2020). "U.S. seizes bitcoin said to be used to finance terrorist groups." *New York Times*, August 13. www.nytimes.com/2020/08/13/us/politics/bitcoin-terrorism.html.

Savell, S. (2021). "United States counterterrorism operations 2018–2020." Cost of War Project, Brown University, February. https://bit.ly/3AVVElD.

Schiemann, J. W. (2012). Interrogational torture: or how good guys get bad information with ugly methods. *Political Research Quarterly*, **65**(1), 3–19.

Schiemann, J. W. (2015). *Does Torture Work?* New York: Oxford University Press.

Schmid, A. P. (1983). *Political Terrorism: A Research Guide to Concepts, Theories, Data Bases, and Literature*. New Brunswick, NJ: Transaction Books.

Schmid, A. P. (1992). Terrorism and democracy. *Terrorism and Political Violence*, **4**(4), 14–25.

Schneider, F., Brück, T., and Meierrieks, D. (2014). The economics of counter-terrorism: a survey. *Journal of Economic Surveys*, **29**(1), 131–157.

Schweich, T. (2006). "Is Afghanistan a narco-state?" *New York Times*, July 27. www.nytimes.com/2008/07/27/magazine/27AFGHAN-t.html?_r&_r=0.

Shughart, W. (2006). An analytical history of terrorism. *Public Choice*, **128**(1), 7–39.

Shughart, W. (2011). Terrorism in rational choice perspective. In C. J. Coyne and R. L. Mathers (eds.) *The Handbook on the Political Economy of War*. Cheltenham: Edward Elgar, pp. 126–154.

Simpson, G. R. (2003). "List of early al Qaeda doners points to Saudi elite, charities." *Wall Street Journal*, March 18. www.wsj.com/articles/SB104794563734573400.

Sidner, S., Rappard, A.-M., and Cohen, M. (2021). "Disproportionate number of current and former military personnel arrested in capitol attack, CNN analysis shows." *CNN*, February 4. www.cnn.com/2021/01/31/us/capitol-riot-arrests-active-military-veterans-soh/index.html.

Slahi, M. O. (2015). *Guantanamo Diary*. New York: Back Bay Books.

Somin, I. (2013). *Democracy and Political Ignorance: Why Smaller Government Is Smarter*. Stanford, CA: Stanford University Press.

Sopko, J. F. (2014). "Future U.S. counternarcotics efforts in Afghanistan." Testimony before the Caucus on International Narcotics Control, U.S. Senate, 113th Congress, 2nd session, January. https://bit.ly/3Myreew.

Sprinzak, E. (2009). "Rational fanatics." *Foreign Policy*, November 20. https://foreignpolicy.com/2009/11/20/rational-fanatics/.

Steinhauer, J. (2015). "With chairmanship, McCain seizes chance to reshape Pentagon agenda." *New York Times*, June 8. https://bit.ly/3ngDqIb.

Stephen, C. (2016). "Libya faces influx of migrants seeking new routes to Europe." *Guardian*, April 9. www.theguardian.com/world/2016/apr/09/libya-influx-migrants-europe.

Storr, V. H. (2008). The market as a social space: on the meaningful extra-economic conversations that can occur in markets. *Review of Austrian Economics*, **21**(2), 135–150.

Storr, V. H., and Choi, G. S. (2019). *Do Markets Corrupt Our Morals?* New York: Palgrave Macmillan.

Storr, V. H., Haeffele-Balch, S., and Grube, L. E. (2015). *Community Revival in the Wake of Disaster: Lessons in Local Entrepreneurship*. New York: Palgrave Macmillan.

Storr, V. H., Haeffele-Balch, S., and Grube, L. E. (2017). Social capital and social learning after Hurricane Sandy. *Review of Austrian Economics*, **30**(4), 447–467.

*Straits Times*. (2017). "Once promised paradise, ISIS fighters end up in mass graves." October 15. https://bit.ly/3LBpyBF.

Sufizada, H. (2020). "The Taliban are megarich – here's where they get the money they use to wage war in Afghanistan." *The Conversation*, December 8. https://bit.ly/3Vi4K5x.

Tarnoff, C. (2012). "Afghanistan: U.S. foreign assistance." Congressional Research Service, Washington, DC. www.hsdl.org/?view&did=723512.

Thrall, A. T., and Cramer, J. K. (eds.). (2009). *American Foreign Policy and the Politics of Fear: Threat Inflation since 9/11*. New York: Routledge.

Tocqueville, A. de (1969). *Democracy in America*, ed. J. P. Mayer, trans. G. Lawrence. New York: Doubleday.

Tullock, G. (1965). *The Politics of Bureaucracy*. Washington, DC: Public Affairs Press.

Twining, D. (2009). "Don't move the goalposts on Afghanistan." *Foreign Policy*, January 28. https://foreignpolicy.com/2009/01/28/dont-move-the-goalposts-on-afghanistan/.

United Nations Office on Drugs and Crime. (2014). "World Drug Report 2014." www.unodc.org/wdr2014/.

United Nations Office on Drugs and Crime. (2020). "World Drug Report 2020." https://wdr.unodc.org/wdr2020/.

United Nations Office on Drugs and Crime. (2021). "Afghanistan Opium Survey 2019." https://bit.ly/3Hj9imo.

United States Court of Appeals for the Ninth Circuit. (2020). *United States v. Moalin*, September 2. https://cdn.ca9.uscourts.gov/datastore/opinions/2020/09/02/13-50572.pdf.

United States Department of Homeland Security. (2003). "Securing the homeland, strengthening the nation." www.dhs.gov/publication/securing-homeland-strengthening-nation.

United States Department of Homeland Security. (2004). "DHS budget in brief – fiscal year 2004." https://bit.ly/3nemMsE.

United States Department of Homeland Security. (2021). "About DHS." www.dhs.gov/about-dhs.

United States Department of State. (2021). "Terrorist designations and state sponsors of terrorism." www.state.gov/terrorist-designations-and-state-sponsors-of-terrorism/.

United States Senate Committee on Appropriations. (2020). "Summary: the department of homeland security fiscal year 2021 appropriations bill." December 21. https://bit.ly/3HnCfgU.

US House Subcommittee on Africa, Global Health, and Human Rights. (2012). "The Tuareg Revolt and the Mali Coup." June 29. www.govinfo.gov/content/pkg/CHRG-112hhrg74863/html/CHRG-112hhrg74863.htm.

Vásquez, I., and McMahon, F. (2020). "The Human Freedom Index 2020: a global measurement of personal, civil and economic freedom." Cato Institute and Fraser Institute. www.cato.org/sites/cato.org/files/2020-12/human-freedom-index-2020.pdf.

Volz, D. (2017). "Most Americans unwilling to give up privacy to thwart attacks: Reuters/Ipsos poll." *Reuters*, April 4. https://bit.ly/3LBVNAK.

Wagner, R. E. (2007). *Fiscal Sociology and the Theory of Public Finance: An Exploratory Essay*. Cheltenham: Edward Elgar.

Wagner, R. E. (2017). *Politics as a Peculiar Business: Insights from a Theory of Entangled Political Economy*. Cheltenham: Edward Elgar.

Wagner, R. E., and Yazigi, D. (2014). Form vs. substance in selection through competition: elections, markets, and political economy. *Public Choice*, **159**(3), 503–514.

Watson Institute for International and Public Affairs at Brown University. (2021). "Costs of war: U.S. costs to date for the war in Afghanistan, in $ billions, 2001–2021." https://bit.ly/449THiK.

Weinberg, L., Pedahzur, A., and Hirsch-Hoefler, S. (2004). The challenges of conceptualizing terrorism. *Terrorism and Political Violence*, **16**(4), 777–794.

Whitlock, C., and Woodward, B. (2016). "Pentagon buries evidence of $125 billion in bureaucratic waste." *Washington Post*, December 5. https://bit.ly/3LDzpa9.

Wintrobe, R. (2006). Can suicide bombers be rational? In *Rational Extremism: The Political Economy of Radicalism*. Cambridge: Cambridge University Press, pp. 108–143.

Wood, G. (2018). The enemy votes: bargaining failure and weapons improvisation. *Economics of Peace and Security Journal*, **13**(1), 25–32.

World Bank. (2020). "Ease of doing business: comparing business regulation in 190 economies." https://bit.ly/3LBVEgG.

World Bank. (2022). "GDP per capita (constant 2015 US$)." https://data.worldbank.org/indicator/NY.GDP.PCAP.KD.

Zakaria, F. (2003). *The Future of Freedom: Illiberal Democracies at Home and Abroad*. New York: W.W. Norton & Company.

Zavadski, K. (2014). "ISIS now has a network of military affiliates in 11 countries around the world." *New York Magazine*, November 23. https://bit.ly/42bRPEt.

Zetter, K. (2020). "How cops can secretly track your phone." *Intercept*, July 31. https://bit.ly/3oUFVAa.

# Acknowledgments

We would like to thank two anonymous reviewers and the editor for useful comments and suggestions for improvement.

*To David R. Henderson –*
*An economist emphasizing the joy of freedom and the wretchedness of war.*

# Cambridge Elements ☰

# Austrian Economics

### Peter Boettke

*George Mason University*

Peter Boettke is a Professor of Economics & Philosophy at George Mason University, the BB&T Professor for the Study of Capitalism, and the director of the F. A. Hayek Program for Advanced Study in Philosophy, Politics and Economics at the Mercatus Center at George Mason University.

## About the Series

This series will primarily be focused on contemporary developments in the Austrian School of Economics and its relevance to the methodological and analytical debates at the frontier of social science and humanities research, and the continuing relevance of the Austrian School of Economics for the practical affairs of public policy throughout the world.

# Cambridge Elements ≡

# Austrian Economics

Printed in the United States
by Baker & Taylor Publisher Services